IBC対訳ライブラリー

英語で読む
江戸川乱歩短篇集

Short Stories of Ranpo Edogawa

著　者：江戸川乱歩
翻訳者：トム・クリスティアン
　　　　モーガン・ジャイルズ
　　　　マット・トライヴォー
イラスト：山田勇男

英 語 解 説 ＝ 久松紀子
ナレーション ＝ David Satterwhite
録音スタジオ ＝ 株式会社巧芸創作

うつし世は夢、
よるの夢こそまこと

山田勇男

　初めて読んだ江戸川乱歩は大正十二年の暮「新青年」に発表された『二銭銅貨』で、厚みのあるその二銭銅貨を二つにはがして、中を浅に空洞にし、雄ネジと雌ネジを刻んで、煉り薬の容器のように、開閉できるものを拵え、その中へ懐中時計のゼンマイにノコギリのような歯をつけたのを隠して、牢屋の鉄格子を挽き切る道具に使う話に、いっぺんに魅了されたのだった。筆名を、敬愛してやまないエドガー・アラン・ポーもじり江戸川藍峯と名乗ってたが『二銭銅貨』発表時、乱歩と改めたそうである。次に読んだのが『木馬は廻る』だった。浅草を舞台に、メリーゴラウンド、人生の残敗者のらっぱ吹き、貧しい少女を配置したノスタルジアに震えた。『パノラマ島綺譚』タイトルが素晴しい。『ひとでなしの恋』は何度も何度も読んだ。『火星の運河』幻想散文詩！とても片寄ったところからの乱歩入門だった。江戸川乱歩の魅力は、夢のような子供っぽい幻想から入って、現実への深い絶望を裏返しにした「もうひとつの、ありえない非日常の世界を人工的につくり出す奇術」の論理がある。眼に見えぬ存在を相手にした、恐怖の快楽と一抹の不安が漂っている。読者諸君！と乱歩は連呼する。「どこの隅を探してみても、もはや、夢も幻も、影さえとどめていない」どんでん返しが待っている。読者諸君！これが怪奇という神秘のヴェールを被った奥底で、断末魔の不気味な笑いを笑っている夢物語なのでございます。

さて、この度の諸作品は大正十四年、乱歩三十歳のころに書かれたもので、どれも代表作ともいうべき好短篇です。『D坂の殺人事件』は、鉄道線路の柵から暗示を受け、縞模様の浴衣と大阪障子の格子をだぶらせ、錯覚を意図した謎解きで、明智小五郎という名探偵が初登場。近代国家の影で誕生した、浪漫怪奇の謎解き探偵明智の存在は、もうひとりの作者自身かも知れないと興味深い。『心理試験』はドストエフスキー『罪と罰』の青年を思い浮かべる。乱歩が神戸の古本屋で見つけた、ミュンスターベルヒの『心理学と犯罪』から、心理学的連想診断法を裏返し、ひっくり返して、犯人のそのトリックを名探偵が発見する話。『人間椅子』は乱歩が夏、籐椅子にもたれ、目の前にあるもう一つの椅子を睨んで、椅子、椅子と口のなかでくりかえしているうちに、椅子の形と人間のしゃがんだ形が似ているなと、大きな肘掛椅子なら人間がはいれて、その上に男や女が腰をかけたら怖いだろう、と夢想されたもの。
　どの結末にもどんでん返しがあって、

「夢物語でよいのだ。
　夢物語でよいのだ」『猟奇の果』

と、夜の夢の異形に憑かれ、苦悩する。はじめっから絶望していたのかも知れない。

ゆえに、虚無の力を信じた乱歩が迷句するあの幻想、
「美しさ身の毛もよだち、恐ろしき歯の根も合わぬ、五彩のオーロラの夢をこそ」
江戸川乱歩の夢は、江戸川乱歩の現実であったのだ。

● 山田勇男　Yamada Isao
1952年、北海道生まれ。
74年、演劇実験室天井棧敷に入団。寺山修司監督作品映画の美術・衣装デザインを担当。
77年、札幌にて漫画家・故湊谷夢吉らと銀河画報社映画倶楽部を結成。稲垣足穂の『一千一秒物語』をモチーフに製作した処女作『スバルの夜』以来、現在まで8mmフィルムを中心に100本を超える作品制作。国内外で特集上映が組まれ、作品は美術館や大学に収蔵されている。
劇場映画の監督作品は、『アンモナイトのささやきを聞いた』(1992、カンヌ国際映画祭招待)、つげ義春原作『蒸発旅日記』(2003)、『シュトルム・ウント・ドランクッ』(2014)。書籍は『夢のフィールド』(1992)、『星のフラグメント』(2003)、『戯れ』(2008)、『人魚』(2013)、『ヤマヴィカ宇宙學』(2014)、『ヤマヴィカ宇宙學II』(2015)がある。

本書の構成

本書は、

- □ 英日対訳による本文
- □ 欄外の語注
- □ 確かな読解のための英語表現
- □ MP3形式の英文音声

で構成されています。

　各ページの下部には、英語を読み進める上で助けとなるよう単語・熟語の意味が掲載されています。また左右ページは、段落のはじまりが対応していますので、日本語を読んで英語を確認するという読み方もスムーズにできるようになっています。また各ストーリーごとに英語解説がありますので、物語を楽しんだ後に、英語の使い方などをチェックしていただくのに最適です。

付属のCD-ROMについて

本書に付属のCD-ROMに収録されている音声は、パソコンや携帯音楽プレーヤーなどで再生することができるMP3ファイル形式です。一般的な音楽CDプレーヤーでは再生できませんので、ご注意ください。

■音声ファイルについて

　付属のCD-ROMには、本書の英語パートの朗読音声が収録されています。本文左ページに出てくるヘッドホンマーク内の数字とファイル名の数字がそれぞれ対応しています。
　パソコンや携帯プレーヤーで、お好きな箇所を繰り返し聴いていただくことで、発音のチェックだけでなく、英語で物語を理解する力が自然に身に付きます。

■音声ファイルの利用方法について

　CD-ROMをパソコンのCD/DVDドライブに入れて、iTunesやx-アプリなどの音楽再生（管理）ソフトにCD-ROM上の音声ファイルを取り込んでご利用ください。

■パソコンの音楽再生ソフトへの取り込みについて

　パソコンにMP3形式の音声ファイルを再生できるアプリケーションがインストールされていることをご確認ください。
　通常のオーディオCDと異なり、CD-ROMをパソコンのCD/DVDドライブに入れても、多くの場合音楽再生ソフトは自動的に起動しません。ご自分でアプリケーションを直接起動して、「ファイル」メニューから「ライブラリに追加」したり、再生ソフトのウインドウ上にファイルをマウスでドラッグ＆ドロップするなどして取り込んでください。
　音声再生ソフトの詳しい操作方法や、携帯音楽プレーヤーへのファイルの転送方法については、ソフトやプレーヤーに付属のマニュアルやオンラインヘルプで確認するか、アプリケーションの開発元にお問い合わせください。

CONTENTS

The Human Chair 9
人間椅子
翻訳：Tom Christian トム・クリスティアン

● 確かな読解のための英語表現　74

The Case of the Murder on D Hill 79
D坂の殺人事件
翻訳：Morgan Giles モーガン・ジャイルズ

● 確かな読解のための英語表現　182

The Psychological Examination 187
心理試験
翻訳：Matt Treyvaud マット・トライヴォー

● 確かな読解のための英語表現　298

The Human Chair
人間椅子

The Human Chair

Every morning, Yoshiko saw her husband off to work at a little after ten o'clock. It was then that she finally had some time for herself, and her habit was to shut herself up in the study—a room which she and her husband both used—in the Western-style wing of their mansion. She was currently working on a long piece of fiction for the special summer edition of K Magazine.

Famous both as a beauty and as an author, Yoshiko's reputation had grown to overshadow that of her husband, a secretary at the Foreign Office. A large number of letters from unknown admirers reached her every day.

Today, too, her first task, after sitting at her desk and before starting her work, was to cast her eye over some letters from complete strangers.

The letters all said the same dull things, as if churned out by rote. With the considerateness and good nature typical of her sex, however, Yoshiko made a point of reading them all through, no matter how dull they were. After all, they were addressed to her.

■off to ～へ出かける　■reputation 图 良い評判　■cast one's eye over ～に目を向ける　■churned out by rote 機械的に大量生産する　■no matter how どんなに～であろうとも

人間椅子

　佳子は、毎朝、夫の登庁を見送ってしまうと、それはいつも十時を過ぎるのだが、やっと自分のからだになって、洋館の方の、夫と共用の書斎へ、とじこもるのが例になっていた。そこで、彼女は今、K雑誌のこの夏の増大号にのせるための、長い創作にとりかかっているのだった。

　美しい閨秀(けいしゅう)作家としての彼女は、この頃では、外務省書記官である夫君の影を薄く思わせるほども、有名になっていた。彼女の所へは、毎日のように未知の崇拝者達からの手紙が、幾通となくやって来た。
　今朝とても、彼女は、書斎の机の前に座ると、仕事にとりかかる前に、まず、それらの未知の人々からの手紙に、目を通さねばならなかった。
　それはいずれも、きまり切ったように、つまらぬ文句のものばかりであったが、彼女は、女の優しい心遣いから、どのような手紙であろうとも、自分に宛られたものは、ともかくも、一通りは読んでみることにしていた。

She began with the simple-looking ones—a couple of regular letters and a post card. After she had read them, what remained was a bulky envelope; Yoshiko suspected that it contained a manuscript. Although she had not received a letter to warn her it was coming, being sent unsolicited manuscripts was nothing unusual for her. The majority were excruciatingly prolix and dull; nevertheless she tore it open and pulled out a stack of pages. "I might as well take a look at the title," she thought to herself.

Just as she had expected, it was a bound bundle of sheets of the square-printed paper favored by writers. Oddly, though, the story featured neither a title nor the name of the author, and the text began abruptly with the word "Madam," directly addressing her. "What's this?" she thought. "So it must be a letter after all." She only needed to run her eyes over the first couple of lines to see that there was something faintly abnormal, even distasteful, about the letter. But her natural curiosity soon got the better of her and she plowed ahead at high speed.

■bulky 形分厚い　■unsolicited 形頼んでいないのに送りつけられた　■excruciatingly 副耐え難いほどに　■prolix 形長ったらしい　■abruptly 副唐突に　■plow ahead 進行していく

簡単なものから先にして、二通の封書と、一葉のはがきとを見てしまうと、あとにはかさ高い原稿らしい一通が残った。別段通知の手紙はもらっていないけれど、そうして、突然原稿を送って来る例は、これまでにしても、よくあることだった。それは、多くの場合、長々しく退屈極る代物であったけれど、彼女はともかくも、表題だけでも見ておこうと、封を切って、中の紙束を取出してみた。

　それは、思った通り、原稿用紙を綴じたものであった。が、どうしたことか、表題も署名もなく、突然「奥様」という、呼びかけの言葉で始まっているのだった。ハテナ、では、やっぱり手紙なのかしら、そう思って、何気なく二行三行と目を走らせていく内に、彼女は、そこから、何となく異常な、妙に気味悪いものを予感した。そして、もちまえの好奇心が、彼女をして、ぐんぐん、先を読ませていくのであった。

The Human Chair

Madam,

I humbly beg your forgiveness. It is wicked for a man whom you have never even met to send you so shameless a letter, out of the blue.

No doubt, Madam, you will be taken aback when I inform you that I intend to confess to you a truly extraordinary crime that I have committed.

I can in all honesty say that for the past several months, I have been living the life of a devil, wholly hidden from the world of men. Not a soul in the wide world knows what I have been up to. Indeed, I might never have returned to the ordinary world of people, had a certain event not taken place.

Recently, however, an astonishing change of heart has taken place within me. It is that which compels me to make this confession about my unfortunate self to you. Much of what I say must strike you as suspicious; nonetheless, I beg you to read this letter through to the end. If you do so, you will understand why I feel as I do, and why I want you in particular, Madam, to hear my confession.

■I humbly beg your forgiveness. なにとぞどうかお許し下さい。 ■out of the blue 突然　■be taken aback ～にびっくりさせられる　■up to（悪事を）もくろんで　■astonishing 形 思いがけない　■nonetheless 副 それでもなお

人間椅子

奥様、

　奥様の方では、少しも御存じのない男から、突然、このようなぶしつけなお手紙を、差上げます罪を、幾重にもお許し下さいませ。

　こんなことを申上げますと、奥様は、さぞかしびっくりなさる事でございましょうが、私は今、あなたの前に、私の犯して来ました、世にも不思議な罪悪を、告白しようとしているのでございます。
　私は数ヵ月の間、全く人間界から姿を隠して、本当に、悪魔のような生活を続けて参りました。もちろん、広い世界に誰一人、私の所業を知るものはありません。もし、何事もなければ、私は、このまま永久に、人間界に立帰ることはなかったかもしれないのでございます。

　ところが、近頃になりまして、私の心にある不思議な変化が起りました。そして、どうしても、この、私の因果な身の上を、懺悔(ざんげ)しないではいられなくなりました。ただ、かように申しましたばかりでは、色々ご不審におぼしめす点もございましょうが、どうか、ともかくも、この手紙を終りまでお読み下さいませ。そうすれば、なぜ、私がそんな気持になったのか。またなぜ、この告白を、ことさら奥様に聞いて頂かねばならぬのか、それらのことが、ことごとく明白になるでございましょう。

The Human Chair

Where should I start? To have to recount so outlandish, so bizarre a story via so prosaic a means as a letter is embarrassing; I can barely bring myself to put pen to paper. Still, dillydallying will do me no good. What I shall do, then, is to start at the beginning and write everything down in the order in which it happened.

I am possessed of a hideously ugly appearance. Do your best to bear that in mind. Should you indulge my boldfaced request and consent to meet with me, it would be hard for me to bear your untutored response to my ugly face—now more loathsome and repulsive than ever due to months of unhealthy living.

I was born under an unlucky star. In spite of my ugly appearance, my heart has always secretly burned with unusually fierce passions. I ignored the reality—that I was no more than a simple craftsman with a face like a monster and dirt poor to boot—and was drawn to sweet dreams of luxury far beyond my social status.

Had I been born into a wealthy family, money, by enabling me to indulge in all kinds of dissipation, might have distracted me from the depressing fact of my ugliness. Had I been endowed with greater artistic talents, composing exquisite poems might have helped me

■outlandish 形異様な　■prosaic 形平凡な　■dillydally 動ぐずぐずする　■loathsome 形いまわしい　■repulsive 形ぞっとする　■dissipation 名気晴らし　■be endowed with ～に恵まれている

さて、何から書き初めたらいいのか、あまりに人間離れのした、奇怪千万な事実なので、こうした、人間世界で使われる、手紙というような方法では、妙におもはゆくて、筆の鈍るのを覚えます。でも、迷っていても仕方がございません。ともかくも、事の起りから、順を追って、書いていくことにいたしましょう。

　私は生れつき、世にも醜い容貌の持主でございます。これをどうか、はっきりと、お覚えなすっていて下さいませ。そうでないと、もし、あなたが、この無躾な願いをいれて、私におあい下さいました場合、たださえ醜い私の顔が、長い月日の不健康な生活のために、ふた目と見られぬ、ひどい姿になっているのを、何の予備知識もなしに、あなたに見られるのは、私としては、たえがたいことでございます。
　私という男は、何と因果な生れつきなのでありましょう。そんな醜い容貌を持ちながら、胸の中では、人知れず、世にもはげしい情熱を、燃していたのでございます。私は、お化のような顔をした、その上ごく貧乏な、一職人に過ぎない私の現実を忘れて、身のほど知らぬ、甘美な、ぜいたくな、種々様々の「夢」にあこがれていたのでございます。
　私がもし、もっと豊かな家に生れていましたなら、金銭の力によって、色々の遊戯にふけり、醜貌（しゅうぼう）のやるせなさを、まぎらすことができたでもありましょう。それともまた、私に、もっと芸術的な天分が、与えられていましたなら、例えば美しい詩歌によって、この世の味気なさを、忘れることができたでもありましょう。しかし、不幸な

The Human Chair

forget the dreariness of life. Unlucky that I am, however, I had no such advantages. I had no choice but to earn my living as a furniture maker, one hard day at a time, doing the job that my father had passed down to me.

Making chairs of any and every kind was my specialty. Even our most demanding clients liked the chairs that I built. As a result, the company singled me out for special treatment, sending all the orders for high-quality pieces in my direction. High quality doesn't just mean carved backrests and armrests; on top of that, there were all sorts of challenging orders based on individual personal preferences about the feel of upholstery or the relative sizes of different parts of the chair. A layperson isn't equipped to imagine just how difficult these orders were to fulfill, but the pleasure of completing them was in direct proportion to the difficulty involved. Would it be presumptuous for me to compare my emotions to the joy that an artist feels upon bringing some magnificent work to completion?

Whenever I finish a chair, the first thing I do is to sit on it to see how it feels. That is the only time in my dreary artisan's life that I get to enjoy a sense of indescribable pride. What noble man or beautiful woman will sit on it

■single ~ out ～を選び出す　■upholstery 图椅子のクッション材　■layperson 图素人　■be equipped to ～の能力がある　■presumptuous 形おこがましい　■dreary 形味気ない

人間椅子

　私は、いずれの恵みにも浴することができず、哀れな、一家具職人の子として、親譲りの仕事によって、その日その日の暮しを、立てていくほかはないのでございました。

　私の専門は、様々の椅子を作ることでありました。私の作った椅子は、どんな難しい注文主にも、きっと気に入るというので、商会でも、私には特別に目をかけて、仕事も、上物ばかりを、まわしてくれておりました。そんな上物になりますと、もたれや肘かけの彫りものに、色々むずかしい注文があったり、クッションのぐあい、各部の寸法などに、微妙な好みがあったりして、それを作る者には、ちょっと素人の想像できないような苦心がいるのでございますが、でも、苦心をすればしただけ、できあがった時の愉快というものはありません。生意気を申すようですけれど、その心持ちは、芸術家が立派な作品を完成した時の喜びにも、比ぶべきものではないかと存じます。

　一つの椅子ができあがると、私はまず、自分で、それに腰かけて、座りぐあいを試してみます。そして、味気ない職人生活の内にも、その時ばかりは、何ともいえぬ得意を感じるのでございます。そこへは、どのような高貴の方が、あるいはどのような美しい方がおかけ

The Human Chair

next? If they were able to order so magnificent a chair, their residence must contain a sumptuous room worthy of it. Oil paintings by celebrated artists must surely line its walls and a chandelier hang from the ceiling like a magnificent jewel. Expensive carpets cover the entire floor. In front of the chair there is a table upon which sit gaudy flowers from the West, emitting a sweet scent and blooming lavishly. As I drifted deeper into my daydream, I imagined that the magnificent room belonged to me and, for the briefest of moments, felt a pleasure that surpasses my powers of description.

These ephemeral fantasies of mine grew unstoppably. Despite being a mere poor, ugly artisan, as I sat in the chair I had made myself, in the world of my dreams I was transformed into a high-minded young nobleman. To one side of me, my beautiful mistress (she always featured in my fantasies) hung on my every word, her face gleaming with smiles. Nor was that all; in my dreams, I held her hand as we whispered sweet nothings to one another.

It never took long, however, before my dreams were interrupted by the jabbering of the local housewives and the hysterical wailing of their sickly children, and sordid reality once again exposed its grey corpse before

★

■sumptuous 形贅沢な　■gaudy 形派手な　■lavishly 副ふんだんに　■surpass 動〜を超える　■ephemeral 形はかない　■jabber 動べちゃくちゃしゃべる　■sordid 形醜い

なさることか、こんな立派な椅子を、注文なさるほどのおやしきだから、そこには、きっと、この椅子にふさわしい、贅沢な部屋があるだろう。かべには定めし、有名な画家の油絵がかかり、天井からは、偉大な宝石のようなシャンデリヤが、さがっているに相違ない。床には、高価なじゅうたんが、敷きつめてあるだろう。そして、この椅子の前のテーブルには、眼のさめるような、西洋草花が、甘美なかおりを放って、咲き乱れていることであろう。そんな妄想にふけっていますと、何だかこう、自分が、その立派な部屋の主にでもなったような気がして、ほんの一瞬間ではありますけれど、何とも形容のできない、愉快な気持になるのでございます。

　私のはかない妄想は、なおとめどもなく増長して参ります。この私が、貧乏な、醜い、一職人に過ぎない私が、妄想の世界では、気高い貴公子になって、私の作った立派な椅子に、腰かけているのでございます。そして、そのかたわらには、いつも私の夢に出て来る、美しい私の恋人が、におやかにほほえみながら、私の話に聞入っております。そればかりではありません。私は妄想の中で、その人と手をとり合って、甘い恋の睦言を、ささやき交しさえするのでございます。
　ところが、いつの場合にも、私のこの、フーワリとした紫の夢は、たちまちにして、近所のおかみさんのかしましい話声や、ヒステリーのように泣き叫ぶ、そのあたりの病児の声にさまたげられて、私の前には、またしても、醜い現実が、あの灰色のむくろをさらけ出す

The Human Chair

me. Returning to reality, I was confronted with my true self: pitiably ugly and with no resemblance to a young nobleman. And as for that beautiful creature who had been smiling at me? Where had she and everything else gone? The squalid nursemaids, dusty from playing with their charges, did not so much as turn to look at me. The only thing that remained from my dream was the chair that I had made. There it stood, stolid and sad. But even it would soon be carted off who knows where to some quite different world to the one I lived in.

In this way, with every new chair I completed, an indescribable sense of life's monotony overcame me. Gradually, that ghastly—that indescribably ghastly—feeling became more than I could bear.

"If I have to live like a maggot, I'd be better off dead," I thought. And I was quite serious. As I diligently plied my chisel, hammered in my nails or mixed up my foul-smelling paints, the same thought went around and around in my head. "Just wait a minute. If you're prepared to face death, mightn't there be another way? For instance...." My thoughts gradually began to take a fearful course.

★

■squalid 形不潔な　■cart off 運び去る　■monotony 名退屈さ　■ghastly 形ひどくいやな　■maggot 名うじ虫　■chisel 名のみ　■foul-smelling 形悪臭のある

のでございます。現実に立帰った私は、そこに、夢の貴公子とは似てもつかない、哀れにも醜い、自分自身の姿を見出します。そして、今の先、私にほほえみかけてくれた、あの美しい人は。……そんなものが、全体どこにいるのでしょう。その辺に、ほこりまみれになって遊んでいる、汚らしい子守女でさえ、私なぞには、見向いてもくれはしないのでございます。ただ一つ、私の作った椅子だけが、今の夢のなごりのように、そこに、ポツネンと残っております。でも、その椅子は、やがて、いずことも知れぬ、私達のとは全く別な世界へ、運び去られてしまうのではありませんか。

　私は、そうして、一つ一つ椅子を仕上げるたびごとに、いい知れぬ味気なさに襲われるのでございます。その、何とも形容のできない、いやあな、いやあな心持は、月日が経つに従って、だんだん、私には堪え切れないものになって参りました。
　「こんな、うじ虫のような生活を、続けていくくらいなら、いっそのこと、死んでしまった方がましだ」私は、真面目に、そんなことを思います。仕事場で、コツコツとのみを使いながら、釘を打ちながら、あるいは、刺激の強い塗料をこねまわしながら、その同じことを、しつように考え続けるのでございます。「だが、待てよ、死んでしまうくらいなら、それほどの決心ができるなら、もっとほかに、方法がないものであろうか。例えば……」そうして、私の考えは、だんだん恐ろしい方へ、向いていくのでありました。

The Human Chair

It was precisely then that I was asked to make some large leather armchairs of a kind I had never previously put my hand to. They were destined for a hotel here in Y City that was managed by a foreign gentleman. They were the kind of thing he would normally have ordered from his home country, but the company for which I worked had managed to win the order by convincing him that craftsmen existed in Japan who were capable of making chairs that were not inferior to those from abroad. That was enough to inspire me: I forgot about the comforts of life and got to work. I toiled obsessively, putting my heart and soul into the job.

Looking at the finished chairs, I felt an unprecedented sense of satisfaction. Though I say it myself, they displayed marvelous and eye-catching workmanship. As was my habit, I dragged one of the four chairs into a wooden-floored room that got plenty of sunshine and plopped myself luxuriantly down. Sitting on it felt wonderful! The pressure of the cushioning—plump but neither too hard nor too soft; the touch of the untreated leather (which I had opted not to dye, leaving it a natural color) against the skin; the opulent backrest, tilted at just the right angle to support the back; the two richly

■be destined for 〜に行くことになっている　■toil 動骨折って働く　■unprecedented 形かつてない　■plop down ドスンと座る　■opt 動〜することに決める　■opulent 形たっぷりとした　■backrest 名背もたれ

ちょうどその頃、私は、かつて手がけたことのない、大きな皮張りの肘掛椅子の、製作を頼まれておりました。この椅子は、同じY市で外人の経営している、あるホテルへ納める品で、一体なら、その本国から取寄せるはずのを、私の雇われていた、商会が運動して、日本にも舶来品に劣らぬ椅子職人がいるからというので、やっと注文を取ったものでした。それだけに、私としても、寝食を忘れてその製作に従事しました。本当に魂をこめて、夢中になってやったものでございます。

　さて、できあがった椅子を見ますと、私はかつて覚えない満足を感じました。それは、我ながら、見とれるほどの、見事なできばえであったのです。私は例によって、四脚一組になっているその椅子の一つを、日当りのよい板の間へ持出して、ゆったりと腰を下しました。何という座り心地のよさでしょう。フックラと、硬すぎずやわらかすぎぬクッションのねばりぐあい、わざと染色を嫌って灰色の生地のまま張りつけた、なめし革の肌触り、適度の傾斜を保って、そっと背中を支えてくれる、豊満なもたれ、デリケートな曲線を描いて、オンモリとふくれ上った、両側の肘掛、それらのすべてが、不思議な調和を保って、渾然として「安楽」という言葉を、そのまま形に現しているようにみえます。

The Human Chair

bulbous armrests with their delicate curves: They were all in perfect accord and struck as the physical expression of the phrase "harmonious comfort."

I was in ecstasy as I sank deep into the chair and squeezed the plump round armrests. Then, as was always the case with me, a series of fantasies spontaneously bubbled unstoppably up, as vivid and as colorful as the many-colored rainbow. They unfurled in front of my eyes, so clear and so true to my imagination, that I feared that I was losing my mind.

As this was going on, a wonderful idea suddenly occurred to me. (I wonder if this is what people mean when they talk about "the devil whispering in one's ear"?) It was as fantastic as a dream and exceedingly perverse. But that very perversity gave it an indescribable appeal which I just could not resist.

At the beginning, it was no more than a simple wish not to let go of the beautiful chair which I had worked so hard on; if I could, I wanted to accompany it wherever it went. As the wish slowly and hypnotically grew inside me, at some point it attached itself to an appalling project that had been festering in my mind lately. Oh, I must be quite mad, for I resolved to put my utterly freakish fantasy into action.

■spontaneously 副自然発生的に ■unfurl 動広げる ■exceedingly 副非常に ■hypnotically 副催眠にかかったように ■appalling 形恐ろしい ■fester 動腐る、膿む ■freakish 形奇怪な

人間椅子

　私は、そこへ深々と身を沈め、両手で、丸々とした肘掛を愛撫しながら、うっとりとしていました。すると、私の癖として、止めどもない妄想が、五色(ごしき)の虹のように、まばゆいばかりの色彩をもって、次から次へとわき上ってくるのです。あれを幻というのでしょうか。心に思うままが、あんまりはっきりと、眼の前に浮んできますので、私は、もしや気でも違うのではないかと、空恐ろしくなったほどでございます。

　そうしています内に、私の頭に、ふとすばらしい考えが浮んで参りました。悪魔の囁きというのは、多分ああした事を指すのではありますまいか。それは、夢のように荒唐無稽(こうとうむけい)で、非常に不気味な事柄でした。でも、その不気味さが、いいしれぬ魅力となって、私をそそのかすのでございます。

　最初は、ただただ、私の丹精をこめた美しい椅子を、手離したくない、できることなら、その椅子と一緒に、どこまでもついていきたい、そんな単純な願いでした。それが、うつらうつらと妄想の翼を拡げております内に、いつの間にやら、その日頃私の頭に醗酵(はっこう)しておりました、ある恐ろしい考えと、結びついてしまったのでございます。そして、私はまあ、何という気違いでございましょう。その奇怪極まる妄想を、実際におこなってみようと思い立ったのでありました。

The Human Chair

I hastily disassembled the handsomest of the four armchairs I had made, then rebuilt it in such a way that I could realize my bizarre plan.

It was an exceptionally large armchair, so the leather-covered base on which you sit almost reached the floor, while the backrest and the arms were unusually broad. Inside it there was a hollow space that ran through the whole thing, such that a man could hide himself in it with no risk of being detected. In this space, I had, of course, installed a sturdy wooden frame and a large number of springs, but a little clever workmanship was all it took for me to create a cavity that was big enough to hide in, provided you sat following the shape of the chair, with your lap beneath the seat and your head and upper body in the backrest.

Since clever adjustments of this kind are my forte, I found it easy enough to reconfigure the chair in a skillful manner. For instance, I made a slit in the leather—quite invisible from the outside—that enabled me to breathe and hear what was going on around me; inside the backrest, right by where my head would be, I also constructed a little shelf for storage and stocked it with a water bottle and some army hardtack. I equipped myself with a large

■hastily 副急いで　■detected 動（存在などに）気づく　■cavity 名空洞
■forte 名得意とするところ　■reconfigure 動再構成する　■hardtack 名乾パン

人間椅子

　私は大急ぎで、四つの内で一番よくできたと思う肘掛椅子を、バラバラにこわしてしまいました。そして、改めて、それを、私の妙な計画を実行するに、都合のよいように造り直しました。
　それは、ごく大型のアームチェーアですから、掛ける部分は、床にすれすれまで皮で張りつめてありますし、そのほか、もたれもひじかけも、非常に部厚にできていて、その内部には、人間一人が隠れていても、決して外から分らないほどの、共通した、大きな空洞があるのです。むろん、そこには、がんじょうな木の枠と、沢山なスプリングが取りつけてありますけれど、私はそれらに、適当な細工を施して、人間が掛ける部分に膝を入れ、もたれの中へ首と胴とを入れ、ちょうど椅子の形に座れば、その中にしのんでいられるほどの、余裕を作ったのでございます。

　そうした細工は、お手のものですから、十分手際よく、便利に仕上げました。例えば、呼吸をしたり外部の物音を聞くために皮の一部に、外からは少しも分らぬような隙間をこしらえたり、もたれの内部の、ちょうど頭のわきの所へ、小さな棚をつけて、何かを貯蔵できるようにしたり、ここへ水筒と、軍隊用の堅パンとを詰め込みました。ある用途のために大きなゴムの袋を備えつけたり、そのほか様々の考案をめぐらして、食料さえあれば、その中に、二日三日はいりつづけていても、決して不便を感じないようにしつらえまし

The Human Chair

rubber bag for certain basic physical needs and came up with various other contrivances, such that, provided I had food, I could stay inside for two or three days without experiencing any inconvenience. The chair now had become a room just right for one person, you might say.

Stripping down to my undershirt, I opened the flap that I had built into the bottom of the chair, and slid inside. It felt strange, I must admit. Pitch dark, hard to breathe, just like being in a tomb—all in all an extraordinary sensation. Come to think of it, it really was like the tomb: the instant that I entered the chair, I had vanished from the world of men, as if I had donned a cloak of invisibility.

A few moments later, one of my fellow employees came around; he was pushing a big handcart to collect the four armchairs. My apprentice—the two of us lived together by ourselves—welcomed him, oblivious as to what was going on. As the laborers loaded up the handcart, one of them growled, "This damn thing weighs a ton!" Inside the chair, I couldn't help giving a start. Still, given that armchairs tend to be heavy things anyway, no one was unduly suspicious and in due course I felt a strange sensation as the thunderous rattling of the cart was transmitted through me.

■come up with 〜を考え出す　■contrivance 名考案　■don 動着用する　■apprentice 名徒弟　■can't help doing どうしても〜してしまう　■give a start ハッとする　■unduly 副過度に

た。いわば、その椅子が、人間一人の部屋になったわけでございます。

　私はシャツ一枚になると、底に仕掛けた出入口のふたを開けて、椅子の中へ、すっぽりと、もぐりこみました。それは、実に変てこな気持でございました。まっ暗な、息苦しい、まるで墓場の中へはいったような、不思議な感じがいたします。考えてみれば、墓場に相違ありません。私は、椅子の中へはいると同時に、ちょうど、隠れみのでも着たように、この人間世界から、消滅してしまうわけですから。

　間もなく、商会から使いのものが、四脚の肘掛椅子を受取るために、大きな荷車を持って、やって参りました。私の内弟子が（私はその男と、たった二人暮しだったのです）何も知らないで、使いのものと応待しております。車に積み込む時、一人の人夫が「こいつは馬鹿に重いぞ」とどなりましたので、椅子の中の私は、思わずハッとしましたが、一体、肘掛椅子そのものが、非常に重いのですから、別段あやしまれることもなく、やがて、ガタガタという、荷車の振動が、私の身体にまで、一種異様の感触を伝えて参りました。

The Human Chair

　I was exceedingly anxious; in the end, though, nothing untoward happened, and the chair with me in it was deposited with a heavy thump in one of the rooms in the hotel that afternoon. It was only later that I found out that this was not a guest bedroom, but a place called a "lounge" where people meet, peruse the newspapers, and smoke cigarettes, with a great variety of characters always coming and going.

　非常に心配しましたけれど、結局、何事もなく、その日の午後には、もう私のはいった肘掛椅子は、ホテルの一室に、どっかりと、据えられておりました。後で分ったのですが、それは、私室ではなくて、人を待合せたり、新聞を読んだり、煙草をふかしたり、色々の人がひんぱんに出入りする、ローンジとでもいうような部屋でございました。

■untoward 形不都合な　■thump 名ドシン（という音）

人間椅子

The Human Chair

I imagine that you have already divined the chief purpose of this eccentric endeavor of mine: to keep watch until no one was about, then to slip out of my chair and prowl around the hotel stealing things. After all, who on earth would ever think of anything so ludicrous as a person hiding in a chair! Like a shadow, I was able to break into one room after another completely at will. As soon as people began to raise a rumpus, I would scoot back to my hidey-hole inside the chair and, taking care to breathe as quietly as I could, amuse myself by watching their nincompoopish attempts to find me. Have you heard of the hermit crab? It's a species of crab that lives on the beach right where the waves break. It looks like a large spider and it struts about as if it owns the place when there's no one nearby. The instant it detects the faintest of footsteps, however, it withdraws into its shell with an extraordinary turn of speed. Then, with just the tiniest length of its disgusting hairy forelegs sticking out of its shell, it watches the movements of its enemy. I was exactly like one of those hermit crabs. My hiding place was a chair rather than a shell, and I swaggered around the hotel rather than a beach.

■eccentric 形奇妙な　■ludicrous 形馬鹿馬鹿しい　■rumpus 名大騒ぎ　■scoot back to 〜へ逃げ帰る　■nincompoopish 形間抜けな　■strut about のさばり歩く　■swagger around ふんぞり返って歩き回る

人間椅子

　もうとっくに、お気づきでございましょうが、私の、この奇妙な行いの第一の目的は、人のいない時を見すまして、椅子の中から抜け出し、ホテルの中をうろつきまわって、盗みを働くことでありました。椅子の中に人間が隠れていようなどと、そんな馬鹿馬鹿しいことを、誰が想像いたしましょう。私は、影のように、自由自在に、部屋から部屋を、荒しまわることができます。そして、人々が、騒ぎ始める時分には、椅子の中の隠家へ逃げ帰って、息をひそめて、彼等の間抜けな捜索を、見物していればよいのです。あなたは、海岸の波打際などに、「やどかり」という一種の蟹のいるのをご存じでございましょう。大きな蜘蛛のようなかっこうをしていて、人がいないと、その辺を我物顔に、のさばり歩いていますが、ちょっとでも人の足音がしますと、恐ろしい速さで、貝殻の中へ逃げ込みます。そして、気味の悪い、毛むくじゃらの前足を、少しばかり貝殻から覗かせて、敵の動静をうかがっております。私はちょうどあの「やどかり」でございました。貝殻の代りに、椅子という隠家を持ち、海岸ではなくて、ホテルの中を、我物顔に、のさばり歩くのでございます。

The Human Chair

Anyway, this outlandish plan of mine, precisely because it was so outlandish, caught everyone off guard and was a marvelous success. By my third day at the hotel, I had already accomplished a great deal. The fear-tinged yet enjoyable feeling that accompanies the carrying out of a robbery, and the indescribable thrill when you manage to pull it off; the amusement to be derived from silently watching people making a commotion right in front of you—"*He went this-a-way!*" "*No, he went that-a-way*": Well, you can probably imagine the extraordinary charm it had for me, and how much entertainment I derived from it.

Unfortunately, though, I do not now have the time to go into such matters in detail. Because this was when I stumbled upon a preeminently bizarre form of pleasure that delighted me ten—nay, twenty—times as much as stealing things. Revealing that to you is the true purpose of this letter.

I need to go back to the beginning and start my story from when my chair was deposited in the hotel lounge.

When the chair was delivered, the hotel managers spent a while testing it for comfort; then everything went quiet; I couldn't hear a thing. I suspect that the room

■fear-tinged 形不安のある　■be derived from 〜から生じる　■commotion 名大騒ぎ　■go into 〜 in detail 〜を詳しく述べる　■preeminently 副極めて　■bizarre 形奇怪な　■nay 間いや、否

さて、この私のとっぴな計画は、それがとっぴであっただけ、人々の意表外にいでて、見事に成功いたしました。ホテルに着いて三日目には、もう、たんまりと一仕事済ませていたほどでございます。いざ盗みをするという時の、恐ろしくも、楽しい心持、うまく成功した時の、何とも形容しがたい嬉しさ、それから、人々が私のすぐ鼻の先で、あっちへ逃げた、こっちへ逃げたと大騒ぎをやっているのを、じっと見ているおかしさ。それがまあ、どのような不思議な魅力を持って、私を楽しませたことでございましょう。

　でも、私は今、残念ながら、それを詳しくお話している暇はありません。私はそこで、そんな盗みなどよりは、十倍も二十倍も、私を喜ばせた所の、奇怪極まる快楽を発見したのでございます。そして、それについて、告白することが、実は、この手紙の本当の目的なのでございます。

　お話を、前に戻して、私の椅子が、ホテルのローンジに置かれた時のことから、始めなければなりません。
　椅子が着くと、ひとしきり、ホテルの主人達が、その座りぐあいをみまわっていきましたが、あとは、ひっそりとして、物音一ついたしません。多分部屋には、誰もいないのでしょう。でも、到着そ

The Human Chair

was deserted. Nonetheless, for a while after my arrival, I was far too frightened to emerge from the chair. For an extremely long time (or perhaps it just felt that way to me) I strained my ears, listening intently to catch any sounds so I could form an idea of what was going on around me.

After a while, I heard the thump-thump-thump (I think it came from the corridor) of someone walking with a heavy tread. The sound came to within five or six yards of me, then became almost inaudible due to the carpet on the floor. A moment later, I heard a man's rough nasal breathing, and before I could even get over my surprise, a large man—it had to be a Westerner—plunked himself down on my lap, then bounced lightly up and down a couple of times. With only a single strip of leather separating my thighs from his magnificent burly buttocks, I was so close that I could feel his bodily warmth. His broad shoulders leaned right up against my chest and his weighty arms overlay mine through the leather. I suppose he must have lit a cigar, for a rich male fragrance came wafting through the slit in the leather.

Try, Madam, to put yourself in my shoes and imagine what is was like. What a truly amazing scene it was! Overcome with terror, I am tightly scrunched up in the

■emerge from ～から出てくる　■tread 图足音　■nasal 图鼻息　■plunk oneself down ドスンと座る　■waft 動フワリとただよう　■put oneself in someone's shoes （人の）立場になって考える　■scrunch up 縮こまる

38

うそう、椅子から出ることなど、とても恐ろしくてできるものではありません。私は、非常に長い間（ただそんなに感じたのかも知れませんが）少しの物音も聞きもらすまいと、全神経を耳に集めて、じっとあたりの様子をうかがっておりました。

　そうして、しばらくしますと、多分廊下の方からでしょう、コツコツと重苦しい足音が響いて来ました。それが、二三間むこうまで近付くと、部屋に敷かれたじゅうたんのために、ほとんど聞きとれぬほどの低い音にかわりましたが、間もなく、荒々しい男の鼻息が聞え、ハッと思う間に、西洋人らしい大きな身体が、私の膝の上に、ドサリと落ちてフカフカと二三度はずみました。私の太ももと、その男のガッシリした偉大な臀部とは、薄いなめし皮一枚を隔てて、あたたかみを感じるほども密接しています。幅の広い彼の肩は、ちょうど私の胸の所へもたれかかり、重い両手は、革を隔てて、私の手と重なり合っています。そして、男がシガーをくゆらしているのでしょう。男性的な、豊なかおりが、革の隙間を通してただよって参ります。

　奥様、仮にあなたが、私の位置にあるものとして、この場の様子を想像してごらんなさいませ。それは、まあ何という、不思議千万な情景でございましょう。私はもう、あまりの恐ろしさに、椅子の

The Human Chair

darkness within the chair, cold sweat pouring from my armpits; the power of thought deserts me; I drift into a stupor.

That man was only the first; throughout the day all sorts of people took turns to sit upon my lap. Not one of them had the least inkling that I was in there or that what they took for comfortable upholstery was in fact a living pair of human thighs.

It was a leather-sheathed world, pitch dark and permitting no movement. Can you imagine how mysterious, yet how appealing a world it was? In it, one perceived human beings as extraordinary creatures, utterly different to the people one sees around one on a daily basis. They are reduced to their voices, their breathing, their footsteps, the rustle of their clothes and a few round, springy lumps of flesh. And I can distinguish them not by their appearance, but by their feel. Someone grossly fat feels like a putrid fish. Contrarily, a gaunt, shriveled person feels like a skeleton. The bend of their spine, the spread of their shoulder blades, the length of their arms, the meatiness of their thighs, the protuberance of their tail bone—take all these together and there is always something different about people, no matter how

■stupor 名放心状態　■inkling 名うすうす感づくこと　■springy 形弾力のある
■putrid 形腐った　■gaunt 形痩せた　■shriveled 形ひからびた
■protuberance 名突起

中の暗闇で、堅く堅く身を縮めて、わきの下からは、冷い汗をタラタラ流しながら、思考力もなにも失ってしまって、ただもう、ボンヤリしていたことでございます。

　その男を手始めに、その日一日、私の膝の上には、色々な人が入り替り立替り、腰を下しました。そして、誰も、私がそこにいることを——彼等が柔いクッションだと信じ切っているものが、実は私という人間の、血の通った太ももであるということを——少しも悟らなかったのでございます。

　まっ暗で、身動きもできない革張りの中の天地。それがまあどれほど、怪しくも魅力ある世界でございましょう。そこでは、人間というものが、日頃目で見ている、あの人間とは、全然別な不思議な生きものとして感ぜられます。彼等は声と、鼻息と、足音と、衣ずれの音と、そして、いくつかの丸々とした弾力に富む肉塊に過ぎないのでございます。私は、彼等の一人一人を、その容貌の代りに、肌触りによって識別することができます。あるものは、デブデブと肥え太って、腐ったさかなのような感触を与えます。それとは正反対に、あるものは、コチコチに痩せひからびて、がいこつのような感じがいたします。そのほか、背骨の曲り方、けんこう骨の開きぐあい、腕の長さ、太ももの太さ、あるいは尾てい骨の長短など、それらのすべての点を総合してみますと、どんな似寄った背かっこうの人でも、どこか違った所があります。人間というものは、容貌や指紋のほかに、こうしたからだ全体の感触によっても、完全に識別することができるに相違ありません。

similar their physiques. There is no doubt that one can identify people based on their overall feel, as well as on their facial appearance and their fingerprints.

The same can also be said about the opposite sex. While under normal circumstances we evaluate them largely based on their looks, that is out of the question in the world within the chair. All you have to go on is their bare flesh, the tone of their voice and their scent.

I hope, Madam, that you will not be offended at the frankness of my account, but it was in the lobby that I developed a powerful physical attachment to a woman. (She was the first woman to ever sit on my chair.)

If I try to picture her based on the sound of her voice, she would be a rather young girl from somewhere abroad. She came in when there was no one else in the room, half-dancing and singing an extraordinary song under her breath as if she had just received some good news. No sooner had I sensed that she was standing in front of the chair in which I was hidden than she flung her voluptuous yet supremely supple body right on top of me. Something must have struck her as funny, for she burst into peals of laughter and clapped her hands and stamped her feet, bouncing around as vigorously as a fish caught in a net.

■bare 形裸の　■scent 名におい　■account 名記述　■attachment 名愛着
■voluptuous 形豊満な　■supple 形しなやかな　■vigorously 副元気に

異性についても、同じことが申されます。普通の場合は、主として容貌の美醜によって、それを批判するのでありましょうが、この椅子の中の世界では、そんなものは、まるで問題外なのでございます。そこには、まる裸の肉体と、声音と、においとがあるばかりでございます。

　奥様、あまりにあからさまな私の記述に、どうか気を悪くしないで下さいまし、私はそこで、一人の女性の肉体に、（それは私の椅子に腰かけた最初の女性でありました。）はげしい愛着を覚えたのでございます。

　声によって想像すれば、それは、まだうら若い異国の乙女でございました。ちょうどその時、部屋の中には誰もいなかったのですが、彼女は、何か嬉しいことでもあった様子で、小声で、不思議な歌を歌いながら、おどるような足どりで、そこへはいって参りました。そして、私のひそんでいる肘掛椅子の前まで来たかと思うと、いきなり、豊満な、それでいて、非常にしなやかな肉体を、私の上へ投げつけました。しかも、彼女は何がおかしいのか、突然アハアハ笑い出し、手足をバタバタさせて、網の中の魚のように、ピチピチとはねまわるのでございます。

The Human Chair

For almost a full half hour, she sat on my knees, occasionally breaking into song and wiggling her heavy figure in time to the music.

To be honest, this unforeseen experience was an earth-shattering event for me. Having regarded women as sacred beings (or maybe more as frightening ones), I had never had the courage to even look at their faces. Now I, of all people, was so close to this unknown foreign girl—not just in the same room and in the same chair, but able to feel the warmth of her skin through a single thin strip of leather. For her part, she felt no awkwardness and was happy to consign her full weight to my knees and behave with the easy-going lack of inhibition that comes from thinking oneself unobserved. I could make as if to hug her from within the chair. Through the leather I could kiss the luscious nape of her neck. I was at complete liberty to do whatever I wanted with her.

As a result of my making this startling discovery, my original goal of theft took a back seat; I was now utterly infatuated with the wonderful world of sensation. I even convinced myself that the within-a-chair world was my naturally ordained habitat. A worthless fellow like me—ugly, weak-willed, tormented by a sense of

★
■wiggle 動クネクネ動く　■inhibition 名抑制　■luscious 形官能的な　■nape 名首筋　■take a back seat 二の次になる　■be infatuated with 〜に夢中になる　■ordain 動〜と定める　■torment 動悩ます

人間椅子

　それから、ほとんど半時間ばかりも、彼女は私の膝の上で、時々歌を歌いながら、その歌に調子をあわせでもするように、クネクネと、重い身体を動かしておりました。
　これは実に、私にとっては、まるで予期しなかった驚天動地の大事件でございました。女は神聖なもの、いやむしろ怖いものとして、顔を見ることさえ遠慮していた私でございます。その私が、今、身も知らぬ異国の乙女と、同じ部屋に、同じ椅子に、それどころではありません、薄いなめし皮一重を隔てて肌のぬくみを感じるほども、密接しているのでございます。それにもかかわらず、彼女は何の不安もなく、全身の重みを私の上に委ねて、見る人のない気安さに、勝手気ままな姿体をいたしております。私は椅子の中で、彼女を抱きしめる真似をすることもできます。皮のうしろから、その豊な首筋に接吻することもできます。そのほか、どんなことをしようと、自由自在なのでございます。

　この驚くべき発見をしてからというものは、私は最初の目的であった盗みなどは第二として、ただもう、その不思議な感触の世界に、惑溺してしまったのでございます。私は考えました。これこそ、この椅子の中の世界こそ、私に与えられた、本当のすみかではないかと。私のような醜い、そして気の弱い男は、明るい、光明の世界では、いつもひけ目を感じながら、恥かしい、みじめな生活を続け

The Human Chair

inferiority—could only live a life of shame and misery in the bright and cheery world outside. Now, by simply changing the environment in which I lived, provided I could endure the cramped conditions within my chair, I could get close to beautiful people—hear their voices, touch their bodies—who would never allow me to approach them, let alone speak to them in the bright world outside.

ていくほかに、能のない身体でございます。それが、ひとたび、住む世界を換えて、こうして椅子の中で、窮屈なしんぼうをしていさえすれば、明るい世界では、口を利くことはもちろん、側へよることさえ許されなかった、美しい人に接近して、その声を聞き肌に触れることもできるのでございます。

■inferiority 名劣等感　■cramped 形窮屈な　■let alone まして~なんて（ない）

人間椅子

The Human Chair

Love inside a chair! It is impossible for anyone who has not actually climbed into a chair to imagine how extraordinary and intoxicating a charm it holds. It is a love comprised only of touch, hearing and a little bit of smell. It is the love of a world of darkness. It is certainly not a love of this world. Perhaps it is the lecherous lust of the devil's own domain. When you stop to think about it, all the aberrant and terrifying things that take place in the nooks and crannies beyond people's notice are truly mind-boggling!

My original plan had been to slip out of the hotel as soon as I had done the stealing I had set out to do; in thrall, however, as I was to a most bizarre form of pleasure, far from getting out of the place, I persisted with my new way of living, resolved to make the interior of the chair my permanent home.

My nightly expeditions involved no danger as I took the utmost care neither to make a sound nor to be seen by anyone. Nonetheless, the fact that I could live inside the chair for several whole months without even coming close to detection came as a surprise even to me.

■intoxicating 形酔わせる　■comprise 動〜から成る　■lecherous 形好色な　■lust 名欲望　■in the nooks and crannies 隅々に　■mind-boggling 形信じられないような　■in thrall 夢中にする　■expedition 名探検

椅子の中の恋（！）それがまあ、どんなに不可思議な、陶酔的な魅力を持つか、実際に椅子の中へいってみた人でなくては、分るものではありません。それは、ただ、触覚と、聴覚と、そしてわずかの嗅覚のみの恋でございます。暗闇の世界の恋でございます。決してこの世のものではありません。これこそ、悪魔の国の愛慾なのではございますまいか。考えてみれば、この世界の、人目につかぬ隅々では、どのように異形な、恐ろしい事柄が、行われているか、ほんとうに想像のほかでございます。

　むろん始めの予定では、盗みの目的を果しさえすれば、すぐにもホテルを逃げ出すつもりでいたのですが、世にも奇怪な喜びに、夢中になった私は、逃げ出すどころか、いつまでもいつまでも、椅子の中を永住のすみかにして、その生活を続けていたのでございます。

　よなよなの外出には、注意に注意を加えて、少しも物音を立てず、また人目に触れないようにしていましたので、当然、危険はありませんでしたが、それにしても、数ヵ月という、長い月日を、そうして少しも見つからず、椅子の中に暮していたというのは、我ながら実に驚くべき事でございました。

The Human Chair

I was spending almost all day, every day in the cramped interior of the chair with my arms and my legs bent. Numb all over and unable to stand upright as a result, I was reduced to scuttling to and fro the kitchen and the bathroom like a crab. I must be insane! For despite all the discomfort I had to endure, I just could not see my way to abandoning that wonderful world of sensation.

For a few of the guests, the hotel was more like a home and they stayed there for a month, sometimes two; still, given the nature of hotels, the majority of people were always coming or going. In consequence, I just had to accept that the objects of my abnormal affections would change as time went by. The memory of my many mistresses was graven in my heart not according to what they looked like, as per the normal way, but primarily according to their physical shape.

One girl was lean and slender and fearless as a filly. Wriggling and writhing wantonly, another had the allure of a snake. Yet another, lavishly endowed with springy fat, was plump as a rubber ball. Another, her body perfectly developed, was hard and strong as a Greek sculpture. Every woman's body had its own distinct charm.

■scuttle 動 ちょこちょこ走る　■to and fro 行ったり来たり　■grave 動（記憶に）刻み付ける　■filly 名 雌の仔馬　■wriggle 動 体をくねらせる　■writhe 動 身をよじる　■wantonly 副 気まぐれに　■allure 名 魅惑

人間椅子

　ほとんど二六時中、椅子の中の窮屈な場所で、腕を曲げ、膝を折っているために、身体中がしびれたようになって、完全に直立することができず、しまいには、料理場や化粧室への往復を、躄のように、這っていったほどでございます。私という男は、何という気違いでありましょう。それほどの苦しみを忍んでも、不思議な感触の世界を見捨てる気になれなかったのでございます。

　中には、一ヵ月も二ヵ月も、そこを住居のようにして、泊りつづけている人もありましたけれど、元来ホテルのことですから絶えず客の出入りがあります。したがって私の奇妙な恋も、時と共に相手が変っていくのを、どうすることもできませんでした。そして、その数々の不思議な恋人の記憶は、普通の場合のように、その容貌によってではなく、主として身体のかっこうによって、私の心に刻みつけられているのでございます。

　あるものは、仔馬のように精悍で、すらりと引き締った肉体を持ち、あるものは、蛇のように妖艶で、クネクネと自在に動く肉体を持ち、あるものは、ゴムまりのように肥え太って、脂肪と弾力に富む肉体を持ち、またあるものは、ギリシャの彫刻のように、ガッシリと力強く、円満に発達した肉体を持っておりました。そのほか、どの女の肉体にも、一人一人、それぞれの特徴があり魅力があったのでございます。

The Human Chair

As I switched like this from one woman to the next, I got to enjoy other extraordinary experiences, of a quite different kind.

One of these involved the ambassador of a Great European Power (I discovered his rank from the gossiping of the Japanese bellboy) who, on one occasion, reposed his noble form upon my lap. Already well known as a politician, he also had a worldwide reputation as a poet. That was reason enough for the opportunity to feel the skin of this great man to give me a thrill of pride. As he sat on top of me, he conducted a roughly ten-minute-long conversation with several of his countrymen before rising to his feet. I didn't, of course, have the faintest idea what he was talking about, but every time he made a gesture, his whole body (which seemed warmer to me than that of the average person) shifted ponderously, galvanizing me in a manner that defies description.

That was when an idea suddenly popped into my head. What sort of effect would I provoke if I made a single deep thrust with a sharp dagger through the leather straight at his heart? It would certainly cause a fatal wound from which he would not recover. What sort of brouhaha would be enacted not just in his home

■repose 動～の上に乗っている　■rise to one's feet 立ち上がる
■ponderously 副重々しく　■galvanize 動～を刺激する　■provoke 動～をひきおこす　■brouhaha 名大騒ぎ

そうして、女から女へと移っていく間に、私はまた、それとは別な、不思議な経験をも味いました。

その一つは、ある時、欧洲のある強国の大使が（日本人のボーイの噂話によって知ったのですが）その偉大な体躯を、私の膝の上にのせたことでございます。それは、政治家としてよりも、世界的な詩人として、一層よく知られていた人ですが、それだけに、私は、その偉人の肌を知ったことが、わくわくするほども、誇らしく思われたのでございます。彼は私の上で、二三人の同国人を相手に、十分ばかり話をすると、そのまま立ち去ってしまいました。むろん、何をいっていたのか、私にはさっぱり分りませんけれど、ジェステュアをする度に、ムクムクと動く、常人よりもあたたかいかと思われる肉体の、くすぐるような感触が、私に一種名状すべからざる刺激を、与えたのでございます。

その時、私はふとこんなことを想像しました。もし！この革のうしろから、鋭いナイフで、彼の心臓を目がけて、グサリと一突きしたなら、どんな結果をひきおこすであろう。むろん、それは彼に再び起つことのできぬ致命傷を与えるに相違ない。彼の本国はもとより、日本の政治界は、そのために、どんな大騒ぎを演じることであろう。新聞は、どんな激情的な記事を掲げることであろう。それは、日本

country, but in Japanese political circles? What sort of impassioned articles would the newspapers run about the event? For sure, his death would be a serious loss for the world, having a serious impact on diplomatic relations between Japan and his country, not to mention from an artistic perspective. With a simple action on my part, I could easily make this grave incident into a reality. At the thought, I could not help feeling quite extraordinarily pleased with myself.

Another episode involved a famous dancer who came to Japan and happened to stay in this hotel and—it was only the one time—sat upon my chair. On that occasion, I felt as moved as I had with the ambassador, but in addition, the dancer transmitted to me a sensation of ideal physical beauty that I had never felt before. So overpowering was her beauty that there was no room in my mind for vulgar thoughts; instead I adored her with the reverence one might direct toward a work of art.

I had many other bizarre, marvelous or perverse experiences. To detail them, however, is not the purpose of this letter, which is already rather on the long side. I should hurry up and get to the main point.

■grave 形重大な ■overpower 動圧倒する ■room 名余地 ■vulgar 形卑しい ■reverence 名崇敬

と彼の本国との外交関係にも、大きな影響を与えようし、また芸術の立場からみても、彼の死は世界の一大損失に相違ない。そんな大事件が、自分の一挙手によって、やすやすと実現できるのだ。それを思うと、私は、不思議な得意を感じないではいられませんでした。

　もう一つは、有名なある国のダンサーが来朝した時、偶然彼女がそのホテルに宿泊して、たった一度ではありましたが、私の椅子に腰かけたことでございます。その時も、私は、大使の場合と似た感銘を受けましたが、その上、彼女は私に、かつて経験したことのない理想的な肉体美の感触を与えてくれました。私はそのあまりの美しさに卑しい考えなどは起すひまもなく、ただもう、芸術品に対する時のような、敬虔な気持で、彼女を讃美したことでございます。

　そのほか、私はまだ色々と、珍しい、不思議な、あるいは気味悪い、数々の経験をいたしましたが、それらを、ここに細叙することは、この手紙の目的でありませんし、それにだいぶ長くなりましたから、急いで、肝心の点にお話を進めることにいたしましょう。

The Human Chair

Several months after I had gotten to the hotel, a change took place in my circumstances. For some reason, the hotel manager had to return to his native country and the hotel was made over as a going concern to a Japanese-run company. Abandoning the hotel's original luxury orientation, the Japanese company planned to make the business more profitable by running it as more of a mass-market, Japanese-style inn. As a result, such furniture as was no longer needed was handed over to a big furniture dealer to be auctioned off. My chair was one of the items to be featured in the auction catalogue.

My first reaction on hearing the news was disappointment. Then I began to think I could use it as an opportunity to return to "the outside" and start life anew. By then, the money I had stolen amounted to a considerable sum, so even if I rejoined the world, I would not have to live the same miserable life as before. Looking back at it now, leaving the foreign-run hotel was a big disappointment in one way, but a new source of hope in another. Let me explain: Despite having fallen in love with such a variety of women over several months, I could not help feeling that something was lacking on the emotional side, because my female counterparts—regardless how

■make over 譲り渡す　■going concern 継続企業　■mass-market 一般向けの　■anew 副もう一度　■female counterpart 女性の恋人

さて、私がホテルへ参りましてから、何ヵ月かの後、私の身の上に一つの変化が起ったのでございます。といいますのは、ホテルの経営者が、何かの都合で帰国することになり、あとを居抜きのまま、ある日本人の会社に譲り渡したのであります。すると、日本人の会社は、従来の贅沢な営業方針を改め、もっと一般向きの旅館として、有利な経営をもくろむことになりました。そのために不用になった調度などは、ある大きな家具商に委託して、競売せしめたのでありますが、その競売目録の内に、私の椅子も加わっていたのでございます。

　私は、それを知ると、一時はガッカリいたしました。そして、それを機として、もう一度しゃばへ立帰り、新しい生活を始めようかと思ったほどでございます。その時分には、盗みためた金が相当の額に上っていましたから、たとい、世の中へ出ても、以前のように、みじめな暮しをすることはないのでした。が、また思い返してみますと、外人のホテルを出たということは、一方においては、大きな失望でありましたけれど、他方においては、一つの新しい希望を意味するものでございました。といいますのは、私は数ヵ月の間も、それほど色々の異性を愛したにもかかわらず、相手がすべて異国人であったために、それがどんな立派な、好もしい肉体の持主であっても、精神的に妙な物足りなさを感じないわけにはいきませんでした。やっぱり、日本人は、同じ日本人に対してでなければ、本当の恋を

The Human Chair

splendid and pleasing their physical attributes—were all foreigners. When push comes to shove, surely a Japanese cannot feel genuine love unless it is toward another Japanese? That was the way my thoughts were tending when my chair was put up for auction. "Perhaps I'll be acquired by a Japanese person. Maybe I'll find a place in a Japanese family." That was my latest aspiration. The upshot was that I decided to continue with my life inside the chair for a little while longer.

I had a dreadful time for several days in the furniture dealer's store. Luckily, though, once the auction got under way, my chair was quick to find a buyer. Although it was now second-hand, the chair was still sufficiently splendid to attract notice.

The buyer was a civil servant who lived in the metropolis not all that far from Y City. Being transported inside the chair on a ferociously shaking truck for many miles from the furniture shop to his residence was so uncomfortable, I thought I was going to die. Still, my discomfort barely deserves a mention in light of the joy I felt at my buyer being, as I had hoped, Japanese.

■attribute 图特質　■when push comes to shove いざとなると　■genuine 形本物の　■aspiration 图強い願望　■upshot 图結論　■get under way 始まる　■ferociously 副ひどく

感じることができないのではあるまいか。私は段々、そんな風に考えていたのでございます。そこへ、ちょうど私の椅子が競売に出たのであります。今度は、ひょっとすると、日本人に買いとられるかもしれない。そして、日本人の家庭に置かれるかもしれない。それが、私の新しい希望でございました。私は、ともかくも、もう少し椅子の中の生活を続けてみることにいたしました。

　道具屋の店先で、二三日の間、非常に苦しい思いをしましたが、でも、競売が始まると、しあわせなことには、私の椅子はさっそく買手がつきました。古くなっても、十分人目を引くほど、立派な椅子だったからでございましょう。

　買手はＹ市からほど遠からぬ、大都会に住んでいた、ある官吏(かんり)でありました。道具屋の店先から、その人の邸まで、何里かの道を、非常に震動のはげしいトラックで運ばれた時には、私は椅子の中で死ぬほどの苦しみをなめましたが、でも、そんなことは、買手が、私の望み通り日本人であったという喜びに比べては、物の数でもございません。

The Human Chair

My civil servant purchaser was the owner of a truly splendid mansion. My chair was deposited in a large study in its Western-style wing. What gave me enormous satisfaction was the fact that the study was used less by the husband and more by his young and beautiful wife. Since arriving here, I have spent roughly a month constantly in her company. Other than when she is eating or sleeping, her supple body is always on top of me. You see, she is always in the study, absorbed in her writing.

This is not the place for me to go on at length about how deeply I fell for her. Not only was she the first Japanese woman I had gotten close to, she was also the possessor of a more than beautiful body. I was truly in love for the first time in my life. In comparison, my many experiences at the hotel were undeserving of the name. The proof of that is, I believe, clear—for with her, I felt something I had never felt before: enjoying secret caresses was no longer adequate and I went to considerable trouble to make her aware of my presence.

If possible, I wanted her to sense that I was inside the chair. And then—I know I'm pushing my luck here—I wanted her to fall in love with me. How could I get that across to her? If I just told her straight out that there was a

■in someone's company 〜と一緒にいて　■be absorbed in 〜に没頭して　■at length 長々と　■undeserving of 〜に値しない　■adequate 形満足のいく　■push one's luck 調子に乗りすぎる　■get ~ across 〜を伝える

買手のお役人は、かなり立派な邸の持主で、私の椅子は、そこの洋館の、広い書斎に置かれましたが、私にとって非常に満足であったことには、その書斎は、主人よりは、むしろ、その家の、若く美しい夫人が使用されるものだったのでございます。それ以来、約一ヵ月の間、私は絶えず、夫人と共におりました。夫人の食事と、就寝の時間を除いては、夫人のしなやかな身体は、いつも私の上にありました。それというのが、夫人は、その間、書斎につめきって、ある著作に没頭していられたからでございます。

　私がどんなに彼女を愛したか、それは、ここにくだくだしく申し上げるまでもありますまい。彼女は、私の始めて接した日本人で、しかも十分美しい肉体の持主でありました。私は、そこに、始めて本当の恋を感じました。それに比べては、ホテルでの、数多い経験などは、決して恋と名づくべきものではございません。その証拠には、これまで一度も、そんなことを感じなかったのに、その夫人に対してだけ私は、ただ秘密の愛撫を楽しむのみではあき足らず、どうかして、私の存在を知らせようと、色々苦心したのでも明かでございましょう。

　私は、できるならば、夫人の方でも、椅子の中の私を意識して欲しかったのでございます。そして、虫のいい話ですが、私を愛してもらいたく思ったのでございます。でも、それをどうして合図いたしましょう。もし、そこに人間が隠れているということを、あからさ

The Human Chair

person hiding inside the chair, she would be sure to tell her husband and the servants out of sheer shock. That would ruin everything; worse, I would also face charges for a heinous crime and be liable for punishment under the law.

I decided that my best bet was to try to make her feel so comfortable in my chair that she developed an affection for it. Artist that she was, she was sure to have a finer sensibility than average. If I could get her to sense the life in my chair and make her love it as a living creature rather than an inanimate object, that would be satisfaction enough for me.

When she flung herself down on top of me, I tried to receive her as softly and gently as I could. When she was sitting on me and was tired, I would slowly and imperceptibly shift my legs to adjust her position. Then, when she finally dozed off and slept, I would play the part of a cradle, jiggling my knees lightly up and down.

I could just be imagining things, but recently I think that my thoughtfulness has been rewarded; the woman seems to have developed a fondness for the chair. She lowers herself into it with the tender sweetness of a baby nestling in its mother's bosom or of a young girl receiving her lover's embrace. I can also detect a sentimental wistfulness in the way she moves upon my lap.

■face charges for ～で告訴される　■heinous 形凶悪な　■inanimate 形生命のない　■imperceptibly 副かすかに　■doze off うとうとする　■jiggle 動軽くゆする　■wistfulness 名物欲しそうな様子

まに知らせたなら、彼女はきっと、驚きのあまり、主人や召使達に、その事を告げるに相違ありません。それではすべてが駄目になってしまうばかりか、私は、恐ろしい罪名を着て、法律上の刑罰をさえ受けなければなりません。

　そこで、私は、せめて夫人に、私の椅子を、この上にも居心地よく感じさせ、それに愛着を起させようと努めました。芸術家である彼女は、きっと常人以上の、微妙な感覚を備えているに相違ありません。もしも、彼女が、私の椅子に生命を感じてくれたなら、ただの物質としてではなく、一つの生きものとして愛着を覚えてくれたなら、それだけでも、私は十分満足なのでございます。

　私は、彼女が私の上に身を投げた時には、できるだけフーワリと優しく受けるように心がけました。彼女が私の上で疲れた時分には、分らぬほどにソロソロと膝を動かして、彼女の身体の位置を換えるようにいたしました。そして、彼女が、うとうとと、居眠りを始めるような場合には、私は、ごくごくかすかに、膝をゆすって、揺籃（ようらん）の役目を勤めたことでございます。

　その心やりが報いられたのか、それとも、単に私の気の迷いか、近頃では、夫人は、何となく私の椅子を愛しているように思われます。彼女は、ちょうど赤ん坊が母親のふところに抱かれる時のような、または、おとめが恋人の抱擁に応じる時のような、甘い優しさをもって私の椅子に身を沈めます。そして、私の膝の上で、身体を動かす様子までが、さも懐しげに見えるのでございます。

Thus it was that my passion burned more fiercely with every passing day. Until finally—Ah, Madam!—until finally, I ended up wishing for something so outrageous as to overstep all bounds of propriety: *If I could just catch just a glimpse of my beloved's face and exchange a word or two with her, I would be happy to die.* That was how far my obsessive thoughts went.

Of course, Madam, I know that you have already figured it out. Forgive my insolence in using the phrase "my lover." The truth is, I mean you. I am the pitiful man who has been so devotedly but hopelessly in love with you ever since your husband purchased my chair at that furniture shop in Y City.

This, Madam, is my dearest wish. Could you not possibly meet with me just once? Could you not then offer a single word of comfort to this pitiable and ugly man? Believe me, I will not ask for more. I am too hideous, too morally tainted to entertain such a hope. I beg you, please, please indulge the ardent prayer of an utterly unhappy man.

I slipped out of your mansion to write this letter last night. Not only would it be very risky for me to make this request face to face, Madam, I simply cannot bring myself to do so.

■end up 結局〜になる　■overstep the bounds of 〜の限度を超える　■catch a glimpse 一目見る　■insolence 名無礼　■taint 動汚れる　■ardent 副熱烈な　■prayer 名祈る人

かようにして、私の情熱は、日々にはげしく燃えていくのでした。そして、遂には、ああ奥様、遂には、私は、身のほどもわきまえぬ、大それた願いを抱くようになったのでございます。たった一目、私の恋人の顔を見て、そして、言葉を交すことができたなら、そのまま死んでもいいとまで、私は、思いつめたのでございます。

　奥様、あなたは、むろん、とっくにお悟りでございましょう。その私の恋人と申しますのは、あまりの失礼をお許し下さいませ。実は、あなたなのでございます。あなたの御主人が、あのＹ市の道具店で、私の椅子をお買取りになって以来、私はあなたに及ばぬ恋をささげていた、哀れな男でございます。

　奥様、一生のお願いでございます。たった一度、私にお逢い下さるわけにはいかぬでございましょうか。そして、一言でも、この哀れな醜い男に、慰めのお言葉をおかけ下さるわけにはいかぬでございましょうか。私は決してそれ以上を望むものではありません。そんなことを望むには、余りに醜く、汚れ果てた私でございます。どうぞどうぞ、世にも不幸な男の、切なる願いをお聞き届け下さいませ。
　私は昨夜、この手紙を書くために、お邸を抜け出しました。面とむかって、奥様にこんなことをお願いするのは、非常に危険でもあり、かつ私にはとてもできないことでございます。

The Human Chair

As you read this letter, I am hovering just outside your house, pale with anxiety.

If you are prepared to grant my most impertinent request, kindly place your handkerchief over the pot of fringed pinks in the window. I shall respond to your signal by going up to the front door of your house, like any ordinary visitor.

This passionate prayer brought the whole extraordinary letter to an end.

Such were Yoshiko's fearful forebodings that by the time she was halfway through it, the blood had quite drained from her face.

Hardly aware of what she was doing, she sprang to her feet and fled from the study with the horrible chair to the living room in the Japanese part of the house. She thought about ripping up the letter and throwing it away without reading it through, but curiosity got the upper hand and she kept on reading at the low desk in the living room.

★

■hover 動 〜のあたりをうろつく　■fringed pink 撫子《植物》　■foreboding 名 悪い予感　■spring to one's feet 飛び上がる　■rip up ビリビリに裂く　■get the upper hand 勝つ

そして、今、あなたがこの手紙をお読みなさる時分には、私は心配のために青い顔をして、お邸のまわりを、うろつきまわっております。
　もし、この、世にも無躾なお願いをお聞き届け下さいますなら、どうか書斎の窓の撫子(なでしこ)の鉢植に、あなたのハンカチをおかけ下さいまし、それを合図に、私は、何気なき一人の訪問者としてお邸の玄関を訪れるでございましょう。

　そして、このふしぎな手紙は、ある熱烈な祈りの言葉をもって結ばれていた。
　佳子は、手紙のなかほどまで読んだ時、すでに恐しい予感のために、まっ青になってしまった。

　そして、無意識に立上ると、気味悪い肘掛椅子の置かれた書斎から逃げ出して、日本建ての居間の方へ来ていた。手紙の後の方は、いっそ読まないで、破りすててしまおうかと思ったけれど、どうやら気がかりなままに、居間の小机の上で、ともかくも、読みつづけた。

The Human Chair

Her fears were justified.

The thought of it was just too terrifying! *A complete and utter stranger had been inside the armchair in which she sat every day of the week.*

"How disgusting!"

She shuddered as though someone had splashed cold water down her back. The trembling would not stop, but went on, seemingly without end.

　彼女の予感はやっぱり当っていた。

　これはまあ、何という恐ろしい事実であろう。彼女が毎日腰かけていた、あの肘掛椅子の中には、見も知らぬ一人の男が、入っていたのであるか。

　「オオ、気味の悪い」

　彼女は、背中から冷水をあびせられたような、悪寒を覚えた。そして、いつまでたっても、不思議な身震いがやまなかった。

■justified 形正当な　■complete and utter 全くの　■disgusting 形気味の悪い

人間椅子

The Human Chair

It was too much to take in. Yoshiko was stupefied; she had no idea what to do. Should she try examining the chair? Could she really bring herself to do something so repulsive? Although the man was no longer inside it, there were sure to be food scraps and other filthy residues of his left behind.

"Madam, a letter for you."

Yoshiko gave a start. Turning, she saw one of the maids bearing a letter which, she said, had just been delivered.

Yoshiko took it automatically; she was just about to open it, when she noticed the inscription and dropped the letter, struck by the most violent and awful surprise. *Her name was in the same hand as the foul letter she had just finished reading!*

For a long time, she could not make up her mind whether or not to open the letter. In the end, she ripped off the seal and read it, her nerves jangling all the while. Although extremely short, the letter was strange enough to give her yet another jolt.

■take in 理解する　■stupefy 動呆然とさせる　■filthy 形汚い　■residue 名残留物　■inscription 名表書き　■foul 形不気味な　■jolt 名ショック

彼女は、あまりのことに、ボンヤリしてしまって、これをどう処置すべきか、まるで見当がつかぬのであった。椅子を調べてみる（？）どうしてどうして、そんな気味の悪いことができるものか。そこにはたとえ、もう人間がいなくても、食物その他の、彼に附属した汚いものが、まだ残されているに相違ないのだ。

「奥様、お手紙でございます」
　ハッとして、振り向くと、それは、一人の女中が、今届いたらしい封書を持て来たのだった。

　佳子は、無意識にそれを受取って、開封しようとしたが、ふと、その上書を見ると、彼女は、思わずその手紙を取りおとしたほども、ひどい驚きに打たれた。そこには、さっきの無気味な手紙と寸分違わぬ筆癖をもって、彼女の名宛が書かれてあったのだ。

　彼女は、長い間、それを開封しようか、しまいかと迷っていた。が、とうとう、最後にそれを破って、ビクビクしながら、中身を読んでいった。手紙はごく短いものであったけれど、そこには、彼女を、もう一度ハッとさせたような、奇妙な文言が記されていた。

The Human Chair

Once again, I must beg your forgiveness for so rudely sending you this letter with no sort of overture. I have been an enthusiastic reader of your masterful work for the longest time. The letter I sent under separate cover was my clumsy attempt at fiction. I would be thrilled if you could look it over and give me your opinion. For reasons of my own, I sent you the manuscript before writing this letter, so I assume that you have already read it. What did you think of it? Nothing would give me greater pleasure than the news that my modest little piece of fiction managed to make an impression upon a master of the art such as yourself.

I deliberately left the title off the manuscript; I am thinking of calling the story "The Human Chair."

With apologies for my rudeness. Sincerely and gratefully yours.

■overture 名申し入れ　■under separate cover 別封で　■clumsy 形つたない
■deliberately 副わざと

人間椅子

　突然お手紙を差上げます無躾を、幾重にもお許し下さいまし。私は日頃、先生のお作を愛読しているものでございます。別封お送り致しましたのは、私のつたない創作でございます。御一覧の上、御批評が頂けますれば、このうえのさいわいはございません。ある理由のために、原稿の方は、この手紙を書きます前に投函いたしましたから、すでに御覧済みかと拝察いたします。いかがでございましたでしょうか。もし、拙作がいくらかでも、先生に感銘を与え得たとしますれば、こんな嬉しいことはないのでございますが。

　原稿には、わざと省いておきましたが、表題は「人間椅子」とつけたい考えでございます。
　では、失礼をかえりみず、お願いまで。匆々(そうそう)。

確かな読解のための英語表現［文法］

いろいろな what

whatには、なんとなく苦手意識があったりしませんか。ここで、きちんと分類して復習しておきましょう。whatには、「whatで始まる疑問文」と「感嘆文」で用いるwhat（疑問代名詞）、what kind of ～など「名詞を修飾する形容詞として働く」what（疑問形容詞）、そして苦手意識のある人の多い関係代名詞があります。ひとつずつ丁寧に見ていきましょう。

> What's this?（p.12, 下から7行目）
> ハテナ。
>
> What did you think of it?（p.72, 下から8行目）
> いかがでございましたでしょうか。

【解説】おなじみの用法からいきましょう。1文目はWhat is this?「これは何ですか」ですね。2文目もWhat do you think of it?は「～についてどう思いますか」と、相手の意見を求める定型表現です。いずれも疑問代名詞のwhatです。

> What a truly amazing scene it was!（p.38, 下から2行目）
> それは、まあ何という、不思議千万な情景でございましょう。

【解説】感嘆文で用いられるwhatです。品詞で言うと、これも疑問代名詞になります。

<u>What</u> noble man or beautiful woman will sit on it next?
（p.18, 一番下）
そこへは、どのような高貴の方が、あるいはどのような美しい方がおかけなさることか。

<u>What</u> sort of effect would I provoke if I made a single deep thrust with a sharp dagger through the leather straight at his heart?（p.52, 下から5行目）
もし！この革のうしろから、鋭いナイフで、彼の心臓を目がけて、グサリと一突きしたなら、どんな結果をひきおこすであろう。

【解説】「どんな〜が」と、名詞を修飾する疑問形容詞のwhatを2つ取り上げてみます。1文目のwhat noble manは「どんな高貴な人」、2文目のwhat sort of effectは「どのような種類の結果」という意味で、どちらも、次に来る名詞にかかる用法です。what sort of 〜と同種の語句としてwhat kind of 〜（意味はいずれも「どんな種類の〜」）があります。

After she had read them, <u>what</u> remained was a bulky envelope;（p.12, 2行目）
（彼女が読んだ）あとにはかさ高い原稿らしい一通が残った。

【解説】いよいよ関係代名詞whatの登場です。whatは先行詞を含んだ関係代名詞で「〜するもの（こと）」が基本的な意味です。ここでは、コンマの後で主語として使われているため、わかりやすいでしょう。

> Not a soul in the wide world knows <u>what</u> I have been up to.
> （p.14, 10行目）
>
> もちろん、広い世界に誰一人、私の所業を知るものはありません。

【解説】knowの後に関係代名詞whatがくることは非常に多いので、英文を読むことに慣れてくると、すぐにピン！と来るでしょう。

ただし、この文は短いわりに読みづらいと感じるかもしれません。その理由のひとつは、文頭の倒置です。not a soul in the worldを強調するために、文の要素としては目的語でありながら文頭に出ています。このように、強調のために否定語を文頭に置くと、倒置が起こります。この文の倒置を元に戻すとA soul in the wide world doesn't know what I have been up to.となります。「誰ひとりとして〜ない」を強調するために Not が a soul（in the world）を伴って文頭に引っ張られたのです。

文末のup toもわかりづらいかもしれません。口語表現で使われる挨拶、What have you been up to?「最近どうしてた？」と同じ意味、用法で、直訳すると「（〜を）して（いた）」となります。

> Not one of them had the least inkling that I was in there or that <u>what</u> they took for comfortable upholstery was in fact a living pair of human thighs.（p.40, 5行目）
>
> そして、誰も、私がそこにいることを——彼等が柔いクッションだと信じ切っているものが、実は私という人間の、血の通った太ももであるということを——少しも悟らなかったのでございます。

【解説】一瞬、文の構造を読み取れずに目が泳いでしまうような文ですが、あわてずに文頭から見ていきましょう。前と同じく、強調の否定語notが文頭に来た倒置表現です。これも倒置なしの文に戻すと、One of them had not least inkling that…「誰一人としてまったく気づかなかった」。notを強調するため、one of themと共に文頭に置かれたのがこの文です。

次に本題のwhatです。what they took for comfortable upholsteryの

take forは、「〜と(誤って)思いこむ」の意味です。

　この文にはもうひとつポイントが隠れています。the least inklingの後と、in there orに続いて、2つthatが置かれていますが、これはinkling that 〜 or that …と読みます。2つとも、inkling「〜に気づくこと」の同格で、inklingの内容を示します。that I was in thereで「私がそこにいること」、that what they took for 〜 .「彼らが〜と思いこんでいるものが…ということ」に「気づくこと」、という意味になります。

> Yoshiko was stupefied; she had no idea what to do.
> (p.70, 1行目)
> 彼女は、ボンヤリしてしまって、これをどう処置すべきか、まるで見当がつかぬのであった。

【解説】関係代名詞の代表的な用法です。have no idea what to do「どうしたらいいのかまったくわからない」は、覚えておいてもいいくらいの頻出表現と言えます。

The Case of the Murder on D Hill
D坂の殺人事件

The Case of the Murder on D Hill

It was a sultry night in early September. I was sipping an iced coffee at the White Plum Blossom Café, a place I often went to near the middle of the main road on D Hill. At the time, I had just left school and had no work to speak of; I spent my days lazing around my boarding house reading books, and when I tired of that, I would go out on aimless walks, making the rounds of cafés that did not cost too much. This was my daily routine. The White Plum Blossom Café was not far from my boarding house, and it was situated such that wherever I walked to I would always pass by it, so it was the café I went to most, but I had the bad habit of lingering too long in any café I entered. And since I have always had a small appetite and little in my purse, I would have two or three cups of cheap coffee and take an hour or two over them, not ordering even one dish of food. Still, it was not that I particularly had taken a liking to any of the waitresses or wanted to harass them. It was better at any rate than

■sultry 形蒸し暑い ■laze around ブラブラと過ごす ■make a round of あちこちの〜を訪れる ■lingering 形長居する ■at any rate 何にしろ

D坂の殺人事件

（上）事実

　それは九月初旬のある蒸し暑い晩のことであった。私は、D坂の大通りの中ほどにある、白梅軒（はくばいけん）という、行きつけのカフェで、冷しコーヒーをすすっていた。当時私は、学校を出たばかりで、まだこれという職業もなく、下宿屋にゴロゴロして本でも読んでいるか、それに飽ると、当てどもなく散歩に出て、あまり費用のかからぬカフェめぐりをやるくらいが、毎日の日課だった。この白梅軒というのは、下宿屋から近くもあり、どこへ散歩するにも、必ずその前を通るような位置にあったので、したがって一番よく出入したわけであったが、私という男は悪い癖で、カフェに入るとどうも長尻（ながっちり）になる。それも、元来食欲の少い方なので、一つは嚢中（のうちゅう）の乏しいせいもあってだが、洋食一皿注文するでなく、安いコーヒーを二杯も三杯もお代りして、一時間も二時間もじっとしているのだ。そうかといって、別段、ウエトレスにおぼしめしがあったり、からかったりするわけではない。まあ、下宿より何となく派手で、居心地がいいのだろう。私はその晩も、例によって、一杯の冷しコーヒーを十分もかかって飲みながら、いつもの往来に面したテーブルに陣取って、ボンヤリ窓の外を眺めていた。

The Case of the Murder on D Hill

my boarding house, and more cheerful. That night I was, as usual, taking my time drinking a cup of iced coffee while stationed at my usual table facing the road, staring absentmindedly out the window.

Now, D Hill, where the White Plum Blossom Café was located and which was previously known for chrysanthemum dolls, had just had its narrow street widened into a broad road called Something Mile Road as part of the urban renewal projects of the Taisho Era, so here and there on both sides of the street were still some empty lots, and at the time of this story it was much lonelier than it is now. Across the road, directly opposite the White Plum Blossom Café, there was a used bookstore. Actually, I had been staring at this storefront for quite some time. As a shabby bookstore on the outskirts of town it was not much to look at, but I had a bit of a special interest in it. That is to say, I had heard from a strange man I had met recently in the White Plum Blossom Café—a man by the name of Akechi Kogoro, an exceedingly odd man to speak to; he seemed intelligent, but the thing which had charmed me about him was his love of detective novels—that a woman who had been his childhood friend was now the wife of the owner of this

■absentmindedly 副上の空で　■chrysanthemum doll 图菊人形《菊の花や葉で衣装をこしらえた人形》　■shabby 形みすぼらしい　■outskirt 图場末

さて、この白梅軒のあるD坂というのは、以前菊人形の名所だった所で、狭かった通りが、市区改正で取拡げられ、何間道路とかいう大通になって間もなくだから、まだ大通の両側にところどころ空地などもあって、今よりずっと淋しかった時分の話だ。大通を越して白梅軒のちょうど真向うに、一軒の古本屋がある。実は私は、先ほどから、そこの店先を眺めていたのだ。みすぼらしい場末の古本屋で、別段眺めるほどの景色でもないのだが、私にはちょっと特別の興味があった。というのは、私が近頃この白梅軒で知合になった一人の妙な男があって、名前は明智小五郎というのだが、話をしてみるといかにも変り者で、それで頭がよさそうで、私の惚れ込んだことには、探偵小説好なのだが、その男の幼馴染の女が今ではこの古本屋の女房になっているという事を、この前、彼から聞いていたからだった。二三度本を買って覚えている所によれば、この古本屋の細君というのが、なかなかの美人で、どこがどういうではないが、何となく官能的に男を引きつけるような所があるのだ。彼女は夜はいつでも店番をしているのだから、今晩もいるに違いないと、店中を、といっても二間半間口の手狭な店だけれど、探してみたが、だれもいない。いずれそのうちに出て来るのだろうと、私はじっと目で待っていたものだ。

bookstore. According to the memories I had of buying books there two or three times, the wife of the bookstore owner was quite a beauty, and although I could not put my finger on what it was exactly, there was something sensual about her which was attractive to men. She was always in charge of the store at night and should have been that night as well, but despite the shop being a small one with only half-width frontage, I looked for her and saw nobody there. Certain that she would come out soon, I waited, watching patiently.

But she did not emerge. Tiring of this, I decided to shift my gaze to the watchmaker's next door. This is when I suddenly noticed that the paper sliding doors with lattice windows that separated the store and the inner rooms were shut tightly. (These sliding doors were of the type which specialists refer to as *muso*, meaning that the central portion which normally would have paper pasted over it was instead made into a narrow, vertical double lattice which could be opened and closed.) Well, that was rather odd indeed. Places like bookstores are very susceptible to shoplifters, so the lattice allowed people inside to keep watch even when they were not in charge of the store, which made it quite strange that the lattice was

■put one's finger on（答えなどを）明確に示す　■in charge of ～を任されて　■frontage 図間口　■paper sliding door 障子　■lattice 図格子戸　■shoplifter 図万引き犯

だが、女房はなかなか出て来ない。で、いい加減面倒臭くなって、隣の時計屋へ目を移そうとしている時であった。私はふと店と奥の間との境に閉めてある障子の格子戸がピッシャリ閉るのを見つけた。──その障子は、専門家の方では無窓(むそう)と称するもので、普通、紙をはるべき中央の部分が、こまかい縦の二重の格子になっていて、それが開閉できるのだ──ハテ変なこともあるものだ。古本屋などというものは、万引されやすい商売だから、たとい店に番をしていなくても、奥に人がいて、障子のすきまなどから、じっと見張っているものなのに、そのすき見の箇所をふさいでしまうとはおかしい、寒い時分ならともかく、九月になったばかりのこんな蒸し暑い晩だのに、第一あの障子が閉切ってあるのから変だ。そんな風に色々考えてみると、古本屋の奥の間に何事かありそうで、私は目を移す気にはなれなかった。

closed. Had it been cold that would be understandable, but it was barely the beginning of September and the night was so sultry that to have those doors closed was odd. As these thoughts went through my mind, I realized it was likely something was going on in the inner rooms, and I did not feel like turning my gaze away any longer.

Speaking of the bookstore owner's wife, I had once heard the waitresses in that café sharing a strange rumor. Although it was just part of their inventory of the ladies and girls they saw in the bathhouse, what I heard them say was: "The mistress of the bookstore is a very pretty lady, but when she's naked, her whole body is covered in bruises—obviously the marks of being beaten and pinched. Her marriage doesn't seem especially bad, either—how strange!" At this point, another woman joined in. "And the mistress of the soba place a few doors down, Asahiya, is often bruised, too. Hers are clearly from being beaten, as well." Now, I did not stop to consider deeply what that bit of gossip might mean, only thinking how cruel their husbands must be, but dear readers, that was not the case at all. Only later did I understand that this trifling matter had an important connection to this whole story.

■turn one's gaze away 目をそらす　■inventory 名 棚卸し　■bruise 名 打撲傷
■pinch 動 つねる　■trifling 形 取るに足らない

古本屋の細君といえば、ある時、このカフェのウエトレス達が、妙な噂をしているのを聞いたことがある。何でも、銭湯で出会うおかみさんや娘達の棚卸しの続きらしかったが、「古本屋のおかみさんは、あんなきれいな人だけれど、はだかになると、身体中傷だらけだ、叩かれたりつねられたりしたあとに違いないわ。別に夫婦仲が悪くもないようだのに、おかしいわねえ」すると別の女がそれを受けて喋るのだ。「あの並びの蕎麦屋の旭屋のおかみさんだって、よく傷をしているわ。あれもどうも叩かれた傷に違いないわ」……で、この、噂話が何を意味するか、私は深くも気に止めないで、ただ亭主が邪険なのだろうくらいに考えたことだが、読者諸君、それがなかなかそうではなかったのだ。ちょっとした事柄だが、この物語全体に大きな関係を持っていることが、後になって分った。

The Case of the Murder on D Hill

At any rate, I stared for over half an hour at the same place. Perhaps you could say it was a premonition, but somehow, I felt that something might happen while I was looking on, and I could not turn my eyes away no matter what. At that moment, Akechi Kogoro, whose name I just mentioned, walked past the window, wearing the same bold, broad-striped *yukata* as always and swinging his shoulders strangely as he walked. Noticing me, he nodded in greeting and came inside. He ordered a cold coffee and sat down next to me facing the window just as I was. Then, realizing that I was looking at one place, he followed my gaze and looked at the same secondhand bookstore opposite. And, curiously, he also seemed truly interested. He stared in that direction without moving his eyes even a little.

While we stared at the same place as if by arrangement, we exchanged all sorts of small talk. As I have now already forgotten what topics we discussed then, and as our conversation has no real connection to the story at hand, I will simply say that I am certain our conversation involved crime and detectives. I will attempt to reproduce a sample of our conversation:

★

■at any rate ともかく　■premonition 虫の知らせ　■look on 〜を見つめる
■no matter what 何があろうと　■at hand 目の前の

それはともかく、そうして、私は三十分ほども同じ所を見詰めていた。虫が知らすとでもいうのか、何だかこう、わき見をしているすきに何事か起りそうで、どうもほかへ目を向けられなかったのだ。そのとき、先ほどちょっと名前の出た明智小五郎が、いつもの荒い棒縞の浴衣を着て、変に肩を振る歩き方で、窓の外を通りかかった。彼は私に気づくと会釈して中へ入って来たが、冷しコーヒーを命じておいて、私と同じように窓の方を向いて、私の隣に腰をかけた。そして、私が一つの所を見詰めているのに気づくと、彼はその私の視線をたどって、同じく向うの古本屋を眺めた。しかも、不思議なことには、彼もまたいかにも興味ありげに、少しも目をそらさないで、その方を凝視し出したのである。

　私達は、そうして、申合せたように同じ場所を眺めながら、色々の無駄話をとりかわした。その時私達の間にどんな話題が話されたか、今ではもう忘れてもいるし、それに、この物語にはあまり関係のないことだから、略するけれど、それが、犯罪や探偵に関したものであったことは確かだ。試みに見本を一つ取出してみると、

The Case of the Murder on D Hill

"It should be impossible to commit a crime that cannot be uncovered, shouldn't it? But I think it is quite possible. Look at Tanizaki Jun'ichiro's *On the Road*. There's no way to detect a crime like that. Of course, in that novel, a detective does discover it, but that was an invention thanks to the author's tremendous power of imagination," said Akechi.

"No, I don't think so. Practical considerations aside, logically speaking, there is no such thing as a crime that cannot be solved. The only thing is, there's no detective on the police force now as great as the one in *On the Road*," I said.

It was that sort of thing. But at one point, we both fell silent as if we had planned it that way. For some time as we had talked, something interesting had been happening at the used bookstore opposite which we had kept our eyes on.

"So you noticed it too," I whispered, and he replied immediately.

"The book thieves, you mean? Very odd, isn't it? I've been watching them since I came in here. This must be the fourth one."

■commit a crime 罪を犯す　■uncover 動 (真相などを) 発見する　■detect 動 〜を発見する　■tremendous 形すばらしい　■keep one's eyes on 〜から目をそらさないでいる

「絶対に発見されない犯罪というのは不可能でしょうか。僕は随分可能性があると思うのですがね。例えば、谷崎潤一郎の『途上』ですね。ああした犯罪はまず発見されることはありませんよ。もっとも、あの小説では、探偵が発見したことになってますけれど、あれは作者のすばらしい想像力が作り出したことですからね」
と明智。

「イヤ、僕はそうは思いませんよ。実際問題としてならともかく、理論的にいって、探偵のできない犯罪なんてありませんよ。ただ、現在の警察に『途上』に出て来るような偉い探偵がいないだけですよ」と私。

ざっとこういった風なのだ。だが、ある瞬間、二人はいい合せたように、黙り込んでしまった。さっきから話しながらも目をそらさないでいた向うの古本屋に、ある面白い事件が発生していたのだ。

「君も気づいているようですね」
と私が囁くと、彼は即座に答えた。
「本どろぼうでしょう。どうも変ですね。僕もここへ入って来た時から、見ていたんですよ。これで四人目ですね」

"You haven't even been here half an hour yet, and there have been four thieves—it is a bit strange. I've been looking over there since before you came in. It was about an hour ago; do you see those sliding doors? I noticed that the lattice part was closed, and I've been paying attention ever since."

"Haven't the people who live there gone out then?"

"But those doors haven't opened even once. If they went out I suppose they could have gone out the back door.... But it is decidedly strange that no one's been there for over half an hour. How about it? Shall we go over there?"

"Yes, let's. Even if nothing bad is going on inside the house, perhaps something else has happened in the store."

I left the café, thinking how interesting it would be if this was a criminal incident. I am sure that Akechi was thinking the very same thing. He, too, was more than a little excited.

The bookstore was of a common type, with a dirt floor throughout the store, bookshelves on the left and far wall stretching nearly from floor to ceiling, with platforms for displaying books at bench height. In the middle of the dirt floor, like an island, there was a rectangular platform for stacking up and displaying books. And just three feet

---

■back door 裏口　■go over 行く　■dirt floor 土間　■platform 陳台
■rectangular 形長方形の　■stack up 〜を積み重ねる

「君が来てからまだ三十分にもなりませんが、三十分に四人も、少しおかしいですね。僕は君の来る前からあすこを見ていたんですよ。一時間ほど前にね、あの障子があるでしょう。あれの格子のようになった所が、閉るのを見たんですが、それからずっと注意していたのです」

「家の人が出て行ったのじゃないのですか」
「それが、あの障子は一度も開かなかったのですよ。出て行ったとすれば裏口からでしょうが、……三十分も人がいないなんて確かに変ですよ。どうです。行ってみようじゃありませんか」

「そうですね。家の中に別状ないとしても、外で何かあったのかも知れませんからね」
　私はこれが犯罪事件ででもあってくれれば面白いと思いながらカフェを出た。明智とても同じ思いに違いなかった。彼も少からず興奮しているのだ。

　古本屋はよくある型で、店全体土間になっていて、正面と左右に天井まで届くような本棚を取付け、その腰の所が本を並べるための台になっている。土間の中央には、島のように、これも本を並べたり積上げたりするための、長方形の台が置いてある。そして、正面の本棚の右の方が三尺ばかりあいていて奥の部屋との通路になり、先にいった一枚の障子が立ててある。いつもは、この障

The Case of the Murder on D Hill

from the right of the bookshelf on the far wall was the passageway to the inner rooms, with the paper door I mentioned earlier. Usually, the master or mistress of the store would be sitting on the tatami mat in front of this door, keeping watch.

Akechi and I walked toward this tatami mat and called out loudly, but there was no reply. It seemed there was no one there. I slid the door open a little and peered inside. The electric light was off and it was pitch black, but a vaguely human form seemed to be lying in the corner. Thinking this was suspicious, I again called out, but they did not answer.

"What the hell, we might as well go in."

So the two of us stepped inside noisily. Akechi twisted the switch for the electric light. At that moment, we both shouted, "Ah!" at the same time. In the corner of the now-bright room lay a woman's corpse.

"It's the mistress of the store," I said eventually. "It looks like she's been strangled, doesn't it?"

Akechi went to her side and examined the body. "There's no chance of resuscitating her at all. We'd better let the police know quickly. I'll go to the public telephone. You keep watch. It would be better if the neighborhood

✦

■peer inside 中を覗く　■pitch black 真っ暗の　■what the hell 仕方ない、何てことだ　■strangle 動 ～を絞め殺す　■resuscitate 動 ～を蘇生させる

子の前の半畳ほどの畳敷の所に、主人か、細君がチョコンと座って番をしているのだ。

　明智と私とは、その畳敷の所まで行って、大声に呼んでみたけれど、何の返事もない。果して誰もいないらしい。私は障子を少し開けて、奥の間を覗いてみると、中は電燈が消えて真暗だが、どうやら、人間らしいものが、部屋の隅に倒れている様子だ。不審に思ってもう一度声をかけたが、返事をしない。

「構わない、上ってみようじゃありませんか」
　そこで、二人はドカドカ奥の間へ上り込んでいった。明智の手で電燈のスイッチがひねられた。そのとたん、私達は同時に「アッ」と声を立てた。明るくなった部屋の片隅には、女の死骸が横わっているのだ。
「ここの細君ですね」やっと私がいった。「首を絞められているようではありませんか」
　明智は側へ寄って死体をしらべていたが、「とても蘇生の見込はありませんよ。早く警察へ知らせなきゃ。僕、自動電話まで行って来ましょう。君、番をしてて下さい。近所へはまだ知らせない方がいいでしょう。手掛りを消してしまってはいけないから」

The Case of the Murder on D Hill

wasn't alerted yet. We mustn't let any clues get destroyed, after all."

Leaving me with these orders, he dashed off to the public telephone, which was located just half a block away.

Although I could hold my own well in an argument about crime or detectives, this was my first time to be confronted with either in reality. I could not do anything. All there was for me to do was just look around the room intently.

彼はこう命令的にいい残して、半町ばかりの所にある自動電話へ飛んで行った。

ふだんから、犯罪だ探偵だと、議論だけはなかなか一人前にやってのける私だが、さて実際にぶっつかったのは初めてだ。手のつけようがない。私は、ただ、まじまじと部屋の様子を眺めているほかはなかった。

■dash off 急行する　■hold one's own 引けを取らない　■be confronted with ～に直面している　■intently 副 ひたすらに

D坂の殺人事件

The Case of the Murder on D Hill

The room was a single six-mat room, and further inside on the right, a narrow porch separated it from the lavatory and a garden no more than sixty-four square feet, with a wooden fence at the back of the garden. (The porch had been left open because it was summer, so I had a clear view.) On the left side of the room was a hinged door, and beyond that was a wood-floored room about two mats in size where I could see a small bathing area next to the back door, a tall paneled wooden door which was closed. On the right side opposite this, there were four sliding screens which were open, and beyond that were the stairs to the second floor and a storeroom. This arrangement was a common one for a cheap row house.

The corpse was near the left wall, lying with her head facing toward the store. To avoid disturbing the scene of the crime, and partly because I felt uneasy, I decided not to approach the body. But the room was small, and as I kept watch, my eyes naturally went in that direction. The woman wore a rough *yukata* with a *chuugata* pattern and lay almost facing upward. Although her clothes were pulled up over her knees, high enough to show her thighs, there were no particular signs of a struggle. I do not know much about these things, but it appeared that her neck was turning purple where she had been strangled.

■hinged door 開き戸 ■sliding screen 障子 ■row house 長屋 ■corpse 死体 ■feel uneasy 気味悪く思う ■lie face upward 仰向けに横たわる

部屋は一間切りの六畳で、奥の方は、右一間は幅の狭い縁側を
へだてて、二坪ばかりの庭と便所があり、庭の向うは板塀になっ
ている。――夏のことで、開けぱなしだから、すっかり、見通し
なのだ、――左半間は開き戸で、その奥に二畳敷ほどの板の間が
あり裏口に接して狭い流し場が見え、そこの腰高障子は閉ってい
る。向って右側は、四枚の襖が閉っていて、中は二階への階段と
物入場になっているらしい。ごくありふれた安長屋の間取だ。

　死骸は、左側の壁寄りに、店の間の方を頭にして倒れている。
私は、なるべく凶行当時の模様を乱すまいとして、一つは気味も
悪かったので、死骸の側へ近寄らないようにしていた。でも、狭
い部屋のことであり、見まいとしても、自然その方に目が行くの
だ。女は荒い中形模様の湯衣を着て、ほとんど仰向きに倒れてい
る。しかし、着物が膝の上の方までまくれて、ももがむき出しに
なっているくらいで、別に抵抗した様子はない。首の所は、よく
は分らぬが、どうやら、絞められたきずが紫色になっているらし
い。

The Case of the Murder on D Hill

There was no end to the people passing by on the road outside. Life went on peacefully and without incident—people talked loudly, their *geta* clapping as they walked, and some drunkenly sang popular songs. Inside the house behind a set of paper doors, a woman had been brutally murdered and lay dead. How ironic. I became strangely sentimental and stood there in a daze.

"They'll be here soon," said Akechi, who was out of breath.

"Right."

Even speaking had become somehow difficult for me. The two of us looked at each other for a long time without speaking a word.

Before long, a policeman in uniform arrived along with a man in a suit. The uniformed man, I later learned, was the chief inspector of K Police Station, and the other man, as one could see from his appearance and what he carried, was a medical officer connected to the same station. We gave the chief inspector a rough explanation of the situation from the beginning. Then, I added this:

"When Akechi here entered the café, I happened to look at the clock. It was precisely half past eight, so I believe the lattice in these doors was probably closed

■pass by そばを通る　■drunkenly 圖酔っ払って　■in a daze 呆然として
■along with ～と一緒に　■happen to 偶然～する

表の大通りには往来が絶えない。声高に話し合って、カラカラと日和下駄(ひよりげた)を引きずって行くのや、酒に酔って流行唄をどなって行くのや、しごく天下泰平なことだ。そして、障子一重の家の中には、一人の女が惨殺されて横わっている。何という皮肉だ。私は妙にセンチメンタルになって、呆然とたたずんでいた。

「すぐ来るそうですよ」
　明智が息を切って帰って来た。
「あ、そう」
　私は何だか口を利くのも大儀(たいぎ)になっていた。二人は長い間、一言もいわないで顔を見合せていた。

　間もなく、一人の正服の警官が背広の男と連立ってやって来た。正服の方は、後で知ったのだが、K警察署の司法主任で、もう一人は、その顔つきや持物でも分るように、同じ署に属する警察医だった。私達は司法主任に、最初からの事情を大略説明した。そして、私はこうつけ加えた。

「この明智君がカフェへ入って来た時、偶然時計を見たのですが、ちょうど八時半頃でしたから、この障子の格子が閉ったのは、恐らく八時頃だったと思います。その時は確か中には電燈がつい

around eight. At that time the electric light inside was definitely on. So it is clear that around eight, at least, there was some living person in this room."

While the chief inspector listened to our statement and took it down in his notebook, the medical officer finished his preliminary examination of the corpse. He waited for us to pause and then he spoke.

"Strangulation. It was done by hand. Take a look at this. Where the skin is turning purple, those are fingerprints. And where she is bleeding is where the fingernails were. Looking at this thumbprint on the right side of her neck, we can see that it was done with a right hand. Let me see... what else? She hasn't been dead for more than an hour, I'd say. But of course, it is too late for resuscitation."

"She appears to have been held down from above," said the chief inspector thoughtfully. "But even so, there's no sign of a struggle.... It must have been done terribly suddenly. And with incredible strength."

Then, he turned toward us and asked us what had happened to the master of the house. But of course, we had no way of knowing. So Akechi, sensibly, called for the owner of the watch store next door.

★
■preliminary 形 予備の　■strangulation 名 絞殺　■fingerprint 名 指の跡、指紋　■let me see ええと、そうですね　■resuscitation 名 蘇生　■have no way of ～ するすべがない

てました。ですから、少くとも八時頃には、だれか生きた人間がこの部屋にいたことは明かです」

　司法主任が私達の陳述を聞取って、手帳に書留めている間に、警察医は一応死体の検診を済ませていた。彼は私達の言葉のとぎれるのを待って言った。

「絞殺ですね。手でやられたのです。これごらんなさい。この紫色になっているのが指のあとです。それから、この出血しているのは爪が当った箇所ですよ。親指のあとが首の右側についているのをみると、右手でやったものですね。そうですね。恐らく死後一時間以上はたっていないでしょう。しかし、無論もう蘇生の見込はありません」

「上から押えつけたのですね」司法主任が考え考え言った。「しかし、それにしては、抵抗した様子がないが……恐らく非常に急激にやったのでしょうね。ひどい力で」

　それから、彼は私達の方を向いて、この家の主人はどうしたのだと尋ねた。だが、無論私達が知っているはずはない。そこで、明智は気を利かして、隣家の時計屋の主人を呼んで来た。

The Case of the Murder on D Hill

The chief inspector's questions and the watch store owner's answers went largely as follows.

"Do you know where the master went to?"

"The master of this store goes out every night to sell books at the night markets, and he usually doesn't come home until around midnight, sir."

"Where are these night markets he sells at?"

"I understand he often goes to Hirokoji in Ueno. As for where he went tonight, unfortunately, I do not know, sir."

"You didn't hear any sounds here an hour ago, did you?"

"What do you mean by 'sounds'?"

"You know what I mean. Like this woman crying out when she was killed, or the sound of a scuffle...."

"I am afraid I did not hear any sounds of that kind."

As this was happening, people in the neighborhood got word and started gathering, and along with curious onlookers who had been passing by, the front of the used bookstore was thronged with people. Among them was also the lady from the *tabi* store on the other side of the bookstore, there to back up the man from the watch shop. She also stated that she had heard no sounds at all.

■scuffle 名格闘　■get word 知る　■onlooker 名見物人　■be thronged with ～で混雑している

司法主任と時計屋の問答は大体次のようなものであった。

「主人はどこへ行ったのかね」
「ここの主人は、毎晩古本の夜店を出しに参りますんで、いつも十二時頃でなきゃ帰って参りません。ヘイ」

「どこへ夜店を出すんだね」
「よく上野の広小路へ参りますようですが。今晩はどこへ出ましたか、どうも手前には分りかねますんで。ヘイ」

「一時間ばかり前に、何か物音を聞かなかったかね」

「物音と申しますと」
「きまっているじゃないか。この女が殺される時の叫び声とか、格闘の音とか……」
「別段これという物音を聞きませんようでございましたが」
　そうこうする内に、近所の人達が聞伝えて集って来たのと、通りがかりの弥次馬で、古本屋の表は一杯の人だかりになった。その中に、もう一方の、隣家の足袋屋のおかみさんがいて、時計屋に応援した。そして、彼女も何も物音を聞かなかったむね陳述した。

During all this, the people of the neighborhood, after consulting amongst themselves, had sent a messenger to where the master of the bookstore was.

Thereupon, I heard a car stop out front and a number of people clomped in to the store. There was a group from the prosecutor's office who had come running because of an urgent message from the police, as well as the chief of K Police Station and Detective Kobayashi, widely reputed as a famous detective then, all of whom had arrived at the same time. (These details and many others I learned afterward, of course, because a friend of mine who was a court reporter was on very friendly terms with Kobayashi, the detective in charge of this case.) The chief inspector, having arrived first, explained the situation so far to these people. We also had to repeat our statements one more time.

"Close the front door."

Suddenly, a man in a black alpaca jacket and white trousers, who looked like a low-level company employee, shouted this order and the door was closed swiftly. This was Detective Kobayashi. Having repelled the rubberneckers thusly, he set upon his investigation. His manner was tremendously arrogant, and he behaved as if

■clomp 動ドスドスと歩く ■prosecutor 名検察官 ■urgent 形緊急の ■reputed 形有名な ■repel 動〜を撃退する ■rubbernecker 名やじ馬 ■thusly 副こんなふうに

この間、近所の人達は、協議の上、古本屋の主人の所へ使いを走らせた様子だった。

　そこへ、表に自動車の止る音がして、数人の人がドヤドヤと入って来た。それは警察からの急報で駈けつけた裁判所の連中と、偶然同時に到着したＫ警察署長、および当時の名探偵という噂の高かった小林刑事などの一行だった。──無論これは後になって分ったことだ、というのは、私の友達に一人の司法記者があって、それがこの事件の係りの小林刑事とごく懇意だったので、私は後日彼から色々と聞くことができたのだ。──先着の司法主任は、この人達の前で今までの模様を説明した。私達も先の陳述をもう一度繰返さねばならなかった。

「表の戸を閉めましょう」
　突然、黒いアルパカの上衣に、白ズボンという、下まわりの会社員みたいな男が、大声でどなって、さっさと戸を閉め出した。これが小林刑事だった。彼はこうして弥次馬を撃退しておいて、さて探偵にとりかかった。彼のやり方はいかにも傍若無人で、検事や署長などはまるで眼中にない様子だった。彼は始めから終りまで一人で活動した。他の人達はただ、彼の敏捷な行動を傍観する

The Case of the Murder on D Hill

the prosecutor and the chief were not there at all. From beginning to end he acted alone. He acted as if the others were mere onlookers, who had come to stand by and watch his deft actions. First, he examined the body. He was especially careful as he turned her neck.

"These finger marks have nothing particularly distinguishing about them. In short, there is also no evidence that anything happened here other than an ordinary human pressing her down with his right hand."

He looked at the prosecutor as he spoke. Next, he suggested temporarily stripping the body. For that, we observers had to be expelled into the shop, as if it were a secret meeting of the Diet. Because of that, I am not certain what was discovered during that time, but in my judgment they must have taken note of the numerous fresh wounds on the deceased's body. These would be the ones the waitresses in the café had been gossiping about.

At last the secret meeting was dismissed, but we refrained from entering the inner room, peering in from the aforementioned tatami mat that divided the shop floor and the back. Fortunately, as we were the people who had discovered the incident and additionally because they later had to take Akechi's fingerprints, we were not

★
■in short つまり　■take note of 〜に注意する　■refrain from 〜を遠慮する
■aforementioned 形 前述の

ためにやって来た見物人に過ぎないようにみえた。彼は第一に死体をしらべた。首のまわりはことに念入りにいじりまわしていたが、

「この指のあとには別に特徴がありません。つまり普通の人間が、右手で押えつけたという以外に何の手掛りもありません」

と検事の方を見て言った。次に彼は一度死体を裸体にしてみるといい出した。そこで、議会の秘密会みたいに、傍聴者の私達は、店の間へ追出されねばならなかった。だから、その間にどういう発見があったか、よく分らないが、察する所、彼等は死人の身体に沢山の生傷のあることに注意したに相違ない。カフェのウエトレスの噂していたあれだ。

やがて、この秘密会が解かれたけれど、私達は奥の間へ入っていくのを遠慮して、例の店の間と奥との境の畳敷の所から奥の方を覗き込んでいた。幸なことには、私達は事件の発見者だったし、それに、後から明智の指紋をとらねばならなかったために、最後まで追出されずに済んだ。というよりは抑留されていたという方が正しいかも知れぬ。しかし小林刑事の活動は奥の間だけに限ら

ejected until the end. Perhaps the correct way to put it is that we were being detained. But because Detective Kobayashi's activities were not just limited to the back room but had a wide range including the outdoors, we had no way to tell the pattern of his investigation from where we stood waiting in one spot. However, luckily for us, the prosecutor camped out in the inner room and barely moved from beginning to end, so as the detectives came and went we got to listen to each of them report on the findings of their investigation without missing out on anything. The prosecutor had his clerk write up the makings of a record on the basis of these reports.

Firstly, a search of the inner room where the body was located had been carried out, but no personal items, footprint, or anything else had caught the detectives' eyes. There was only one exception.

"There are fingerprints on the switch for the electric light," said the detective, sprinkling some kind of white powder on the black Ebonite switch. "Considering the order of the circumstances, whoever turned off the light must have been the culprit. But which one of you turned it on?"

Akechi replied that it had been he.

✦

■eject 勔追い出す　■camp out 陣取る　■carry out 実行する　■ebonite 図エボナイト、硬質ゴム　■culprit 図犯人

れていたわけでなく、屋内屋外の広い範囲にわたっていたのだから、一つ所にじっとしていた私達に、その捜査の模様が分ろうはずがないのだが、うまいぐあいに、検事が奥の間に陣取っていて、始終ほとんど動かなかったので、刑事が出たり入ったりするたびに、いちいち捜査の結果を報告するのを、洩れなく聞きとることができた。検事はその報告にもとづいて、調書の材料を書記に書きとめさしていた。

　まず、死体のあった奥の間の捜索が行われたが、遺留品も、足跡も、その他探偵の目に触れる何物もなかった様子だ。ただ一つのものを除いては。

「電燈のスイッチに指紋があります」黒いエボナイトのスイッチに何か白い粉をふりかけていた刑事がいった。「前後の事情から考えて、電燈を消したのは犯人に相違ありません。しかしこれをつけたのはあなた方のうちどちらですか」

　明智は自分だと答えた。

The Case of the Murder on D Hill

"I see. Please let us take your fingerprints later. Take care not to touch the electric light; we'll dismount it to take with us."

Then, the detective went up to the second floor and did not come back down for a while, but when he did come down, he went outside immediately saying he needed to take a look at the alley. That took him perhaps ten minutes. In good time he returned, the flashlight in his hand still on, bringing with him a man. He was a filthy man, barely forty, dressed in a dirty crepe shirt and khaki trousers.

"There's almost no point looking for footprints," the detective reported. "Near this back door there is an awful lot of mud because it gets very little sun, and it is a jumble of *geta* tracks, so it is very difficult to untangle the situation. By the way, this man," he said, pointing at the man he had just brought with him, "runs an ice cream store on the corner where this alley comes out. The alley has one outlet, so if the culprit did run out the back, this man must have seen him. You, answer my questions once more."

Thereafter, the ice cream man was questioned by the detective.

★

■take care 気をつける　■alley 图路地　■filthy 形汚い　■no point 無駄である
■track 图足跡　■untangle 動解決する

「そうですか。あとであなたの指紋をとらせて下さい。この電燈は触らないようにして、このまま取はずして持っていきましょう」

　それから、刑事は二階へ上っていってしばらく下りてこなかったが、下りてくるとすぐに路地をしらべるのだといって出ていった。それが十分もかかったろうか、やがて、彼はまだついたままの懐中電燈を片手に、一人の男を連れて帰って来た。それは汚れたクレップシャツにカーキ色のズボンといういでたちで、四十ばかりの汚い男だ。

「足跡はまるで駄目です」刑事が報告した。「この裏口の辺は、日当りが悪いせいかひどいぬかるみで、下駄の跡が滅多無性についているんだから、とても分りっこありません。ところで、この男ですが」と今連れて来た男を指し「これは、この裏の路地を出た所の角に店を出していたアイスクリーム屋ですが、もし犯人が裏口から逃げたとすれば、路地は一方口なんですから、必ずこの男の目についたはずです。君、もう一度私の尋ねることに答えてごらん」

　そこで、アイスクリーム屋と刑事の問答。

The Case of the Murder on D Hill

"Did anyone come or go down this alley around eight o'clock tonight?"

"Not one person, and since it became dark, not so much as a kitten has passed by here." The ice cream man was rather good at answering to the point.

"I've been running a shop here for a long time, and even the ladies in these row houses rarely go through here at night. Anyway, the alley takes you through places with bad footing, and it's pitch black."

"Did any of the customers of your shop go into the alley?"

"No, they did not. Everyone ate their ice cream in front of me and went straight back the way they came. Of that I am certain."

Well, if the testimony of this ice cream man was to be trusted, even if the culprit had run off through the back door of the house, he did not come out of the alley which was the only path from the back door. That said, he hadn't gone out through the front either, because we had been watching it from the White Plum Blossom Café. So what precisely had happened to him? According to Detective Kobayashi's thinking, either the culprit could have been hiding out in one of the row houses which

★

■kitten 图子猫　■with bad footing 足場の悪い　■testimony 图証言　■run off 逃げ去る　■hide out 潜伏している

「今晩八時前後に、この路地を出入したものはないかね」

「一人もありませんので、日が暮れてからこっち、猫の子一匹通りませんので」アイスクリーム屋はなかなか要領よく答える。

「私は長らくここへ店を出させてもらってますが、あすこは、この長屋のおかみさん達も、夜分は滅多に通りませんので、何分あの足場の悪い所へ持ってきて、真暗なんですから」

「君の店のお客で路地の中へ入ったものはないかね」

「それもございません。皆さん私の目の前でアイスクリームを食べて、すぐ元の方へお帰りになりました。それはもう間違いはありません」

　さて、もしこのアイスクリーム屋の証言が信用すべきものだとすると、犯人はたとえこの家の裏口から逃げたとしても、その裏口からの唯一の通路である路地は出なかったことになる。さればといって、表の方から出なかったことも、私達が白梅軒から見ていたのだから間違いはない。では彼は一体どうしたのであろう。小林刑事の考えによれば、これは、犯人がこの路地を取りまいている裏表二側の長屋の、どこかの家に潜伏しているか、それとも借家人の内に犯人があるのかどちらかであろう。もっとも二階から屋根伝いに逃げる路はあるけれど、二階をしらべた所によると、

The Case of the Murder on D Hill

lined both sides of the alley, or one of the tenants was the culprit. Although there was a way to escape along the roofs from the second story, upon investigation of the second story the front windows had lattices fitted which did not seem to have been moved in the slightest. The windows at the back of all the houses on the second floor were left open in that heat, and inside were people hanging up their washing, so it seemed that it would have been a little difficult to escape that way. So that was that.

The investigators had a consultation amongst themselves about how to proceed with their investigation, and eventually they decided to split up and go door to door through the area. I say that, but there were only eleven houses on either side of the alley, so it was not much trouble for them. At the same time, the interior of the house was examined again from underneath the porch up to the eaves, in every nook and cranny. But not only did this not bear any fruit, it rather appeared to complicate matters. That is to say, it was found that the owner of the confectionary store next to the used bookstore had been up on his roof where clothes were set to dry, playing his *shakuhachi* from sunset until a few moments ago, and from beginning to end he had been

★

■story 名（建物の）階　■split up（人数が）分かれる　■eave 名ひさし、軒
■every nook and cranny くまなく　■confectionary 名菓子類

表の方の窓は取りつけの格子がはまっていて少しも動かした様子はないのだし、裏の方の窓だって、この暑さでは、どこの家も二階は明けっぱなしで、中には物干で涼んでいる人もあるくらいだから、ここから逃げるのはちょっと難しいように思われる。とこういうのだ。

　そこで臨検者達の間に、ちょっと捜査方針についての協議が開かれたが、結局、手分けをして近所を軒並にしらべてみることになった。といっても、裏表の長屋を合せて十一軒しかないのだから、大して面倒ではない。それと同時に家の中も再度、縁の下から天井裏まで残るくまなくしらべられた。ところがその結果は、何の得る処もなかったばかりでなく、かえって事情を困難にしてしまったようにみえた。というのは、古本屋の一軒おいて隣の菓子屋の主人が、日暮れ時分からつい今し方まで屋上の物干へ出て尺八を吹いていたことが分ったが、彼は始めから終いまで、ちょうど古本屋の二階の窓の出来事を見逃すはずのないような位置に座っていたのだ。

The Case of the Murder on D Hill

sitting in a position where he could not have failed to see anything that happened with the windows on the second story of the used bookstore.

Dear readers, the case had become quite interesting. Where had the culprit come in, and from where had he escaped? It could not have been by the back door, it could not have been by the second-story windows, and it could not have been by the front, of course. Had he not existed from the beginning, or had he disappeared like smoke? And these were not the only mysteries. A pair of students that Detective Kobayashi brought in front of the prosecutor gave truly strange statements. They were students at a technical school who were renting one of the row houses behind the store, and neither of them appeared to be the kind of man to talk nonsense, but nonetheless their statements were of such a nature that they made the incident more and more inexplicable.

In response to the prosecutor's questions, their answers were roughly as follows.

"Around eight o'clock, I was standing in the front of this used bookstore and I had opened up a magazine on that table and was looking at it. Then, because I heard a noise from the back, I suddenly looked up toward these

■nonetheless 副それにもかかわらず　■nature 名性質　■inexplicable 形不可解な　■open up 広げる

読者諸君、事件はなかなか面白くなってきた。犯人はどこから入って、どこから逃げたのか、裏口からでもない、二階の窓からでもない、そして表からでは勿論ない。彼は最初から存在しなかったのか、それとも煙のように消えてしまったのか。不思議はそればかりでない。小林刑事が、検事の前に連れて来た二人の学生が、実に妙なことを申立てたのだ。それは裏側の長屋に間借りしている、ある工業学校の生徒達で、二人共でたらめをいうような男ともみえぬが、それにもかかわらず、彼等の陳述は、この事件をますます不可解にするような性質のものだったのである。

　検事の質問に対して、彼等は大体左(さ)のように答えた。

「僕はちょうど八時頃に、この古本屋の前に立って、そこの台にある雑誌を開いて見ていたのです。すると、奥の方で何だか物音がしたもんですから、ふと目を上げてこの障子の方を見ますと、障子は閉まっていましたけれど、この格子のようになった所が開

The Case of the Murder on D Hill

shoji, but they had been closed. However, this lattice-like part was open, so through the gap I could see a man standing there. But just as I raised my eyes the man shut the lattice, so of course I cannot give more details, however I am certain that it was a man because of his belt."

"Did you notice anything else about him, other than that he was a man? His height, or the pattern of his kimono?"

"I saw him from the waist down, so I don't know about his height, but his kimono was black. Perhaps it had thin stripes or a dye pattern. But to my eyes it looked plain black."

"I was with my friend looking at books," said the other student. "And I became aware of a noise, the same as him, and I saw the lattice shut, the same as him. But the man was definitely wearing a white kimono. It was a pure white kimono, no stripes or pattern."

"Isn't that odd? One of you must be mistaken."

"I certainly am not mistaken."

"Nor am I telling a lie."

■gap 図すき間　■other than 〜以外の　■pattern 図柄　■dye pattern 絣《染織模様の一種》

いてましたので、そのすき間に一人の男の立っているのが見えました。しかし、私が目を上げるのと、その男が、この格子を閉めるのとほとんど同時でしたから、詳しいことは無論分りませんが、でも、帯のぐあいで男だったことは確かです」

「で、男だったというほかに何か気づいた点はありませんか、背格好とか、着物の柄とか」

「見えたのは腰から下ですから、背格好はちょっと分りませんが、着物は黒いものでした。ひょっとしたら、細い縞か絣(かすり)であったかもしれませんけれど。私の目には黒無地に見えました」

「僕もこの友達と一緒に本を見ていたんです」ともう一方の学生、「そして、同じように物音に気づいて同じように格子の閉るのを見ました。ですが、その男は確かに白い着物を着ていました。縞も模様もない、真白な着物です」

「それは変ではありませんか。君達の内どちらかが間違いでなけりゃ」
「決して間違いではありません」
「僕も嘘はいいません」

The Case of the Murder on D Hill

I imagine that my clever readers will have probably already realized something about what these two students' mysterious statements meant. In fact, I realized it myself. However, the people from the prosecutor's office and the police did not seem to think too deeply on this point.

この二人の学生の不思議な陳述は何を意味するか、鋭敏な読者は恐らくあることに気づかれたであろう。実は、私もそれに気づいたのだ。しかし、裁判所や警察の人達は、この点について、余りに深く考えない様子だった。

D坂の殺人事件

The Case of the Murder on D Hill

Soon, the husband of the deceased, the bookseller, heard the news and came back. He was a delicate young man and did not look like a used bookseller, and when he saw his wife's corpse, his weakness was apparent and he could not speak, but tears spilled down his face. Detective Kobayashi waited for the man to settle down, then began to question him. The prosecutor also chipped in. But to their disappointment, he said that he had no idea who the culprit could be. "There is no one that holds this kind of grudge against us," he said, crying. And after making certain checks himself, he confirmed that no robber had been at work there. Thereafter, he was interrogated about his history, his wife's background, and about other matters, but there were no particular points of suspicion, and as this interrogation has no major relevance to the plot of this story I will omit it. Finally, the detective asked about the many fresh wounds on the body of the deceased. The husband was extremely hesitant, but eventually he said that he had inflicted them. However, he would not give a very clear reason for doing so, no matter how he was coaxed and questioned. But because it was known that he was out the entire evening selling at the night market, he could not be suspected of her murder

■deceased 名 故人　■chip in 口を挟む　■grudge 名 怨恨　■interrogate 動 尋問する　■omit 動 省略する　■inflict 動 (傷などを) 負わせる　■coax 動 〜するよう説得する

間もなく、死人の夫の古本屋が、知らせを聞いて帰って来た。彼は古本屋らしくない、きゃしゃな、若い男だったが、細君の死骸を見ると、気の弱いたちとみえて、声こそ出さないけれど、涙をぼろぼろこぼしていた。小林刑事は、彼が落着くのを待って、質問を始めた。検事も口を添えた。だが、彼等の失望したことは、主人は全然犯人の心当りがないというのだ。彼は「これに限って、人様に怨みを受けるようなものではございません」といって泣くのだ。それに、彼が色々調べた結果、物とりの仕業でないことも確められた。そこで、主人の経歴、細君の身元そのほか様々の取調べがあったけれど、それらは別段疑うべき点もなく、この話の筋に大した関係もないので略することにする。最後に死人の身体にある多くの生傷について刑事の質問があった。主人は非常に躊躇しておったが、やっと自分がつけたのだと答えた。ところが、その理由については、くどく訊ねられたにも拘らず、余り明白な答は与えなかった。しかし、彼はその夜ずっと夜店を出していたことが分っているのだから、たとえそれが虐待の傷痕だったとしても、殺害の疑いはかからぬはずだ。刑事もそう思ったのか、深くせんさくしなかった。

The Case of the Murder on D Hill

even if those were marks of mistreatment. The detective must have thought so too, for he did not pry too deeply.

With that, the night's investigation was over for the time being. Our names, addresses, and so on were jotted down, Akechi's fingerprints were taken, and by the time we headed home it was already past one.

If nothing had been missed in the police's search, and it was assumed also that the witnesses were not lying, then this really was a mysterious case. And moreover, according to what I later learned, all of Detective Kobayashi's investigations that he continued to carry out from the next day onward were of no use, and not a bit of progress was made with the case after the night it happened. The witnesses were all trustworthy people. There was nothing suspicious about the residents of the eleven row houses. Inquiries were made in the victim's hometown, but there was nothing strange there either. At least, after Detective Kobayashi (the man who was widely known as a famous detective, as I said before) had searched with all his might, all he could do was conclude that the case was utterly inexplicable. Later I heard that, discouragingly, they could not find anything other than Akechi's fingerprints on the electric light switch, the only

✦
　■jot down 〜を書き留める　■from the day onward その日以来　■inquiry 名 取り調べ　■discouragingly 副 落胆したことに

そうして、その夜の取調べはひとまず終った。私達は住所姓名などを書留められ、明智は指紋をとられて、帰途についたのは、もう一時を過ぎていた。

　もし警察の捜索に手抜かりがなく、また証人達も嘘を言わなかったとすれば、これは実に不可解な事件であった。しかも、後で分った所によると、翌日から引続いて行われた、小林刑事のあらゆる取調べも何の甲斐もなくて、事件は発生の当夜のまま少しだって発展しなかったのだ。証人達はすべて信頼するに足る人々だった。十一軒の長屋の住人にも疑うべき所はなかった。被害者の国許も取調べられたけれど、これまた、何の変った事もない。少くとも、小林刑事――彼は先にもいった通り、名探偵と噂されている人だ――が、全力を尽して捜索した限りでは、この事件は全然不可解と結論するほかはなかった。これもあとで聞いたのだが、小林刑事が唯一の証拠品として、頼みをかけて持帰った例の電燈のスイッチにも、落胆したことには、明智の指紋のほか何物も発見することができなかった。明智はあの際で慌てていたせいか、そこには沢山の指紋が印せられていたが、すべて彼自身のものだった。恐らく、明智の指紋が犯人のそれを消してしまったのだろうと、刑事は判断した。

The Case of the Murder on D Hill

piece of evidence that Kobayashi had requested to take away. There were lots of fingerprints on the switch, but they all belonged to Akechi, perhaps because he was in a hurry at that time. The detective decided that Akechi's fingerprints had probably erased those of the culprit.

Dear readers, I wonder if reading this story you are reminded of Poe's *The Murders in the Rue Morgue* or Doyle's *The Adventure of the Speckled Band.* In other words, I wonder if you are imagining that the culprit in this murder case is not a human but something like an orangutan or a venomous snake from India. I actually thought this myself. However, it was unthinkable that such things could be in the area of D Hill in Tokyo, and in the first place, there were witnesses who said that they had seen a man through the shoji. Not only that, but were it an ape or something similar, there was no way it would not have left footprints and it would have also attracted people's attention. Furthermore, the finger marks on the neck of the deceased were surely those of a human. Had a snake wound itself around her neck, it would not have left that kind of mark.

★

■Poe 名（エドガー・アラン・）ポー《アメリカの作家》　■Doyle 名（アーサー・コナン・）ドイル《イギリスの作家》　■venomous 形 毒を持つ　■in the first place まず第一に

読者諸君、諸君はこの話を読んで、ポオの「モルグ街の殺人」やドイルの「スペックルド・バンド」を連想されはしないだろうか。つまり、この殺人事件の犯人は、人間でなくて、オランウータンだとか、インドの毒蛇だとかいうような種類のものだと想像されはしないだろうか。私も実はそれを考えたのだ。しかし、東京のD坂あたりにそんなものがいるとも思われぬし、第一障子のすき間から、男の姿を見たという証人がある。のみならず、猿類などだったら、足跡の残らぬはずはなく、また人目にもついたはずだ。そして、死人の首にあった指のあとも、正に人間のそれだ。蛇がまきついたとて、あんなあとは残らぬ。

The Case of the Murder on D Hill

Anyway, as Akechi and I returned to our homes that evening, we spoke on many matters with great excitement. To give an example, this was the sort of thing we discussed:

"You must know of the Rose Delacourt case in Paris which became the source for Poe's *The Murder in the Rue Morgue* and Leroux's *The Mystery of the Yellow Room*. Even today, over one hundred years later, there are still mysteries remaining about that strange murder case. I am reminded of it. Isn't tonight's case, with a culprit who vanishes without a trace, somewhat similar?" said Akechi.

"You're right. It really is strange. People often say that the kind of serious crime found in foreign detective novels does not happen in Japanese-style buildings, but I certainly don't think that's the case. Because this sort of incident does indeed happen. I feel that, although I don't know if I could investigate it or not, somehow I'd like to give it a shot with this case," I said.

After that we parted ways at a certain alley. I remember seeing Akechi turn down that alleyway, with his characteristic way of shaking his shoulders while he walked, and the way that his bold, block stripe *yukata* stood out in the darkness as his retreating figure quickly walked home.

★

■Leroux 名（ガストン・）ルルー《フランスの作家》 ■vanish 動姿を消す ■give it a shot 一丁やってみる ■stand out くっきりと浮き出る

それはともかく、明智と私とは、その夜帰途につきながら、非常に興奮して色々と話合ったものだ。一例を上げると、まあこんな風なことを。

「君はポオの『ル・モルグ』やルルーの『黄色の部屋』などの材料になった、あのパリーの Rose Delacourt 事件を知っているでしょう。百年以上たった今日でも、まだ謎として残っているあの不思議な殺人事件を。僕はあれを思出したのですよ。今夜の事件も犯人の立去った跡のない所は、どうやら、あれに似ているではありませんか」と明智。

「そうですね。実に不思議ですね。よく、日本の建築では、外国の探偵小説にあるような深刻な犯罪は起らないなんていいますが、僕は決してそうじゃないと思いますよ。現にこうした事件もあるのですからね。僕は何だか、できるかできないか分りませんけれど、一つこの事件を探偵してみたいような気がしますよ」

　そうして、私達はある横町で分れを告げた。そのとき私は、横町を曲って、彼一流の肩を振る歩き方で、さっさと帰って行く明智の後姿が、その派手な棒縞の浴衣によってやみの中にくっきりと浮出して見えたのを覚えている。

The Case of the Murder on D Hill

The Solution

Well, one day, about ten days after the murder, I called in on Akechi Kogoro's lodgings. During those ten days, what had Akechi and I done, thought, and concluded about the case? Readers may be able to judge that sufficiently based on the conversation that was exchanged between Akechi and myself that day.

I had only seen Akechi in the café until then, and this was my first time calling upon him at his lodgings, but because I had asked him about the place before, I had no difficulty in finding it. I stood in front of a tobacconist which seemed like it might be the place and asked the lady of the shop whether Akechi was in or not.

"Yes, he's in. Please wait, I'll call for him now."

Saying this, she went to the foot of a staircase which I could see from the storefront and called loudly for Akechi. He rented the second story of this house. Then:

"Oh...."

■call in on ちょっと〜を訪ねる　■sufficiently 副 十分に　■tobacconist 名 煙草屋　■whether 〜 or not 〜かそれとも〜でないか

D坂の殺人事件

（下）推理

　さて、殺人事件から十日ほどたったある日、私は明智小五郎の宿を訪ねた。その十日の間に、明智と私とが、この事件に関して、何を為し、何を考えそして何を結論したか。読者は、それらを、この日、彼と私との間に取交された会話によって、十分察することができるであろう。

　それまで、明智とはカフェで顔を合していたばかりで、宿を訪ねるのは、その時が始めてだったけれど、かねて所を聞いていたので、探すのに骨は折れなかった。私は、それらしい煙草屋の店先に立って、おかみさんに、明智がいるかどうかを尋ねた。

「エエ、いらっしゃいます。ちょっとお待ち下さい、今お呼びしますから」
　彼女はそういって、店先から見えている階段の上り口まで行って、大声に明智を呼んだ。彼はこの家の二階を間借りしているのだ。すると、
「オー」

With this strange reply, Akechi came down the creaking stairs, but upon discovering me there, he looked surprised and said, "Come right up." I followed him up to the second floor. However, when I nonchalantly took a single step into his room, I gasped in astonishment. The state of his room was just too strange. I was not unaware of the fact that Akechi was an eccentric, but this was just too eccentric.

The modest, four and a half mat—sized room was filled with books. A little of the tatami was visible only in the center of the room, but the rest was covered by mountains of books piled along the sliding doors and walls in each direction, their bases filling nearly the entire room and their peaks narrowing as they almost reached the ceiling, forming embankments of books on all sides. He had no other furniture. It was enough to make me wonder just how he managed to sleep in there. In the first place, there was nowhere for my host and me to sit, and any careless movement would have sent the books tumbling down at once, possibly crushing us.

"It is very cramped, and on top of that, I have no floor cushions. I'm sorry. Please find a soft-looking book to sit on top of."

■creak 動ミシミシときしむ　■nonchalantly 副何気なく　■in astonishment びっくりして　■embankment 名土手　■tumble down 崩れ落ちる　■cramped 形狭い

と変な返事をして、明智はミシミシと階段を下りて来たが、私を発見すると、驚いた顔をして「ヤー、お上りなさい」といった。私は彼の後に従って二階へ上った。ところが、何気なく、彼の部屋へ一歩足を踏み込んだ時、私はアッとたまげてしまった。部屋の様子があまりにも異様だったからだ。明智が変り者だということを知らぬではなかったけれど、これはまた変り過ぎていた。

　何のことはない、四畳半の座敷が書物で埋まっているのだ。真中の所に少し畳が見えるだけで、あとは本の山だ、四方の壁や襖に沿って、下の方はほとんど部屋一杯に、上の方ほど幅が狭くなって、天井の近くまで、四方から書物の土手が迫っているのだ。ほかの道具などは何もない。一体彼はこの部屋でどうして寝るのだろうと疑われるほどだ。第一、主客二人の座る所もない、うっかり身動きしようものなら、たちまち本の土手くずれで、おしつぶされてしまうかも知れない。

「どうも狭くっていけませんが、それに、座蒲団がないのです。すみませんが、柔かそうな本の上へでも座って下さい」

The Case of the Murder on D Hill

I forced my way into the mountains of books and eventually found somewhere to sit. Overwhelmed, I looked around vacantly for a while.

I must venture to set out here an explanation of Akechi Kogoro, the master of this very eccentric room. Because our friendship was a recent one, I was not at all certain of many things about him—his background, how he made his living, what his goal in life was, and so on—but what was certain was that he was some sort of idler without any particular profession. At a guess I would have said he was a student, but he would have made an exceptionally strange one. He had once told me, "I am studying humanity," but at that time I did not really know what he meant. However, what I did know was that he had an extraordinary interest in crime and detectives and a fearsome wealth of knowledge.

He was about the same age as me and could not have been more than twenty-five years old. If I had to say, he was a thin man and, as I said earlier, he had a strange way of shaking his shoulders when he walked, which brought to mind Kanda Hakuryu, the professional storyteller with one disabled arm, although I do not mean to say Akechi was one of the greats, only to offer a comparison for

■force one's way into 〜に分け入る　■venture to あえて〜する　■at a guess 推測で　■exceptionally 副 並外れて　■comparison 名 類似

私は書物の山に分け入って、やっと座る場所を見つけたが、あまりのことに、しばらく、ぼんやりとそのあたりを見まわしていた。
　私は、かくも風変りな部屋の主である明智小五郎のひととなりについて、ここで一応説明しておかねばなるまい。しかし彼とは昨今のつき合いだから、彼がどういう経歴の男で、何によって衣食し、何を目的にこの人世を送っているのか、というようなことは一切分らぬけれど、彼が、これという職業を持たぬ一種の遊民であることは確かだ。しいていえば書生であろうか、だが、書生にしてはよほど風変りな書生だ。いつか彼が「僕は人間を研究しているんですよ」といったことがあるが、そのとき私には、それが何を意味するのかよく分らなかった。ただ、分っているのは、彼が犯罪や探偵について、並々ならぬ興味と、恐るべく豊富な知識を持っていることだ。

　年は私と同じくらいで、二十五歳を越してはいまい。どちらかといえばやせた方で、先にもいった通り、歩く時に変に肩を振る癖がある、といっても、決して豪傑流のそれではなく、妙な男を引合いに出すが、あの片腕の不自由な、講釈師の神田伯龍を思出させるような歩き方なのだ。伯龍といえば、明智は顔つきから声音まで、彼にそっくりだ、──伯龍を見たことのない読者は、諸君の知っている内で、いわゆる好男子ではないが、どことなく愛

The Case of the Murder on D Hill

this strange man. Speaking of Hakuryu, Akechi was his spitting image from his face to his voice. (Readers who have never seen Hakuryu should imagine, from what they know, a man who would not be called handsome, but one with the face of a genius, and a rather charming one at that.) Only, Akechi's hair was much longer and more disheveled. And he had the habit of running his fingers through his disheveled hair, often while he was talking to people, making it even more ruffled. He did not seem to care about clothing in the slightest, and he always wore a cotton kimono, cinched with a shabby-looking sash.

"Thank you so much for calling on me. I haven't seen you since then. How is the D Hill case getting on? It doesn't look like the police have much hope of catching the criminal, does it?"

Akechi ran his fingers through his hair in the way I mentioned before, while staring at my face intently.

"The truth is, I came today because I have something to discuss with you about that," I started, unsure of how to raise the subject.

■spitting image うり二つ　■disheveled 形 だらしなく乱れた　■cinch 動 締める　■sash 名 帯、サッシュ　■get on 進行する

嬌のある、そして最も天才的な顔を想像するがよい――ただ明智の方は、髪の毛がもっと長く延びていて、モジャモジャともつれ合っている。そして、彼は人と話している間にもよく、指で、そのモジャモジャになっている髪の毛を、更らにモジャモジャにするためのようにひっかきまわすのが癖だ。服装などは一向構わぬ方らしく、いつも木綿の着物に、よれよれの兵児帯を締めている。

「よく訪ねてくれましたね。その後しばらく会いませんが、例のD坂の事件はどうです。警察の方では一向犯人の見込がつかぬようではありませんか」

明智は例の、頭を掻まわしながら、ジロジロ私の顔を眺めていう。

「実は僕、今日はそのことで少し話があって来たんですがね」そこで私はどういう風に切り出したものかと迷いながら始めた。

The Case of the Murder on D Hill

"I've been thinking about a lot of things since then. Not just thinking—I've also made my own investigations at the scene, like a detective. And as a matter of fact, I've come to one conclusion. I thought that I should inform you of it...."

"Oh, that's splendid. I should like to hear all the details."

I did not miss the tinges of contempt and relief that appeared in his eyes, as if to say, "What could you know about it?" This spurred on my hesitant spirit. I steeled myself and began to talk.

"One of my friends is a newspaper reporter, and he's close to Kobayashi, the detective in charge of the case. And through this reporter I was able to learn in detail about the state of the police investigation, but it seems that their methods have gotten them nowhere. Of course, they're trying all sorts of things, but they have no particular leads. Take that electric light switch—it's useless, too. They found that the only fingerprints on it were yours. The police think it's likely that your fingerprints covered over those of the criminal. That is why, since I learned that the police are stuck, I felt that I should investigate the case even more earnestly. Now, what conclusion do you think I have reached, and why do

■at the scene 現場で　■splendid 形すてきな　■contempt 名軽蔑　■spur on 激励する　■steel oneself 勇気を出す　■get ~ nowhere ~に何ももたらさない

「僕はあれから、種々考えてみたんですよ。考えたばかりでなく、探偵のように実地の取調べもやったのですよ。そして、実は一つの結論に達したのです。それを君にご報告しようと思って……」

「ホウ。そいつはすてきですね。詳しく聞きたいものですね」

　私は、そういう彼の目付に、何が分るものかというような、軽蔑と安心の色が浮んでいるのを見逃さなかった。そして、それが私の逡巡している心を激励した。私はいきおいこんで話し始めた。

「僕の友達に一人の新聞記者がありましてね、それが、例の事件の係りの小林刑事というのと懇意なのです。で、僕はその新聞記者を通じて、警察の模様を詳しく知ることができましたが、警察ではどうも捜査方針が立たないらしいのです。無論いろいろ活動はしているのですが、これという見込がつかぬのです。あの、例の電燈のスイッチですね。あれも駄目なんです。あすこには、君の指紋だけっきゃついていないことが分ったのです。警察の考えでは、多分君の指紋が犯人の指紋を隠してしまったのだというのですよ。そういうわけで、警察が困っていることを知ったものですから、僕は一層熱心に調べてみる気になりました。そこで、僕が到達した結論というのは、どんなものだと思います、そして、それを警察へ訴える前に、君の所へ話しに来たのは何のためだと思います。

The Case of the Murder on D Hill

you think I have come to speak with you before going to the police?

"Nevertheless, there's something I have realized since the day of the incident. You must remember it too. I am speaking of the completely different accounts that the two students gave regarding the color of the suspected criminal's clothing. One said it was black, and the other said that it was white. However uncertain the human eye may be, is it not strange that they were able to mistake such opposite colors as black and white? I do not know in what way the police have interpreted it, but I believe that neither student's statement was mistaken. Do you see? The criminal was wearing clothing with black and white stripes.... In other words, a *yukata* with thick black stripes. The sort often rented out by inns.... So if you ask why it looked solid white to one person and solid black to another, this is because they saw it through the gap in the lattice of the shoji, and at just that second one student was in a position to see a white part of the kimono through the gap, and the other was in a position to see the black part. Although this is an unusual coincidence, it is by no means impossible. And I can think of no other way to explain the situation.

■nevertheless 副 このような次第ではあるが　■account 名 説明　■interpret 動 解釈する　■coincidence 名 (偶然の)一致

それはともかく、僕はあの事件のあった日から、あることを気づいていたのですよ。君は覚えているでしょう。二人の学生が犯人らしい男の着物の色について、まるで違った申立てをしたことをね。一人は黒だといい、一人は白だというのです。いくら人間の目が不確だといって、正反対の黒と白とを間違えるのは変じゃないですか。警察ではあれをどんな風に解釈したか知りませんが、僕は二人の陳述は両方とも間違でないと思うのですよ。君、分りますか。あれはね、犯人が白と黒とのだんだらの着物を着ていたんですよ。……つまり、太い黒の棒縞の浴衣なんかですね。よく宿屋の貸浴衣にあるような……では何故それが一人に真白に見え、もう一人には真黒に見えたかといいますと、彼等は障子の格子のすき間から見たのですから、ちょうどその瞬間、一人の目が格子のすき間と着物の白地の部分と一致して見える位置にあり、もう一人の目が黒地の部分と一致して見える位置にあったんです。これは珍らしい偶然かも知れませんが、決して不可能ではないのです。そして、この場合こう考えるよりほかに方法がないのです。

The Case of the Murder on D Hill

🎧10 "Now, we know that the culprit wore a striped kimono, and this can be said to narrow the range of our investigation, but we still have nothing definite. The second ground for my argument is the fingerprints on the electric light switch. Using my friend, the newspaper reporter I spoke of before, I asked Detective Kobayashi to inspect those fingerprints—your fingerprints—very closely. The result confirmed beyond a doubt that I am not mistaken in my thinking. By the way, would you be so good as to loan me an inkstone for a moment, if you have one?"

Then, I tried an experiment. First borrowing the inkstone, I put a thin layer of ink on my right thumb and pressed a single fingerprint on a piece of writing paper from my pocket. Next, I waited for the fingerprint to dry, then put ink on the same finger again and carefully pressed it down again over the first print, this time changing my finger's direction. When I did this, the tangled double layers of both fingerprints were clearly visible.

"The police's explanation is that your fingerprints were on top of the culprit's and erased them, but as we can see from this experiment now that is impossible. No matter

★

■loan 動貸す　■inkstone 名すずり　■tangled 形もつれた　■visible 形一目瞭然の

さて、犯人の着物の縞柄は分りましたが、これでは単に捜査範囲が縮小されたというまでで、まだ確定的のものではありません。第二の論拠は、あの電燈のスイッチの指紋なんです。僕は、さっき話した新聞記者の友達のつてで、小林刑事に頼んでその指紋を――君の指紋ですよ――よくしらべさせてもらったのです。その結果いよいよ僕の考えてることが間違っていないのを確めました。ところで、君、硯があったら、ちょっと貸してくれませんか」

　そこで、私は一つの実験をやってみせた。まず硯を借りる、私は右の親指に薄く墨をつけて、懐から半紙の上に一つの指紋をおした。それから、その指紋の乾くのを待って、もう一度同じ指に墨をつけ前の指紋の上から、今度は指の方向を換えて念入りに押えつけた。すると、そこには互に交錯した二重の指紋がハッキリ現れた。

「警察では、君の指紋が犯人の指紋の上に重って、それを消してしまったのだと解釈しているのですが、しかしそれは今の実験でも分る通り不可能なんですよ。いくら強く押した所で、指紋とい

how hard you press down, fingerprints are made up of lines, and between the lines there should still be traces of the previous fingerprints. If the previous fingerprints were exactly the same as the new ones and their placement also did not differ at all, then each line of the fingerprints would match, or the new fingerprints might also cover the previous ones, but such a thing is unbelievable first of all, and even if it were true it would not change my conclusion in this case.

"However, if the culprit was the one who turned off the light, he must have left his fingerprints on the switch. I wondered if the police might have overlooked the earlier fingerprints that remained between the lines of your fingerprints, and I tried examining it myself, but there was not the slightest trace. In short, the only fingerprints on that switch, both before and after, were yours. As for why there were no fingerprints from the people at the secondhand bookstore, I do not know, but perhaps the light in that room was always left on, and had never been turned off.

"So what does this all mean? My thinking goes like this. A man wearing a kimono with rough stripes, a man who could be the childhood friend of the dead woman

■make up of ～を構成する　■overlook 動見落とす　■secondhand 形中古の

うものが線でできている以上、線と線との間に、前の指紋の跡が残るはずです。もし前後の指紋が全く同じもので、捺し方も寸分違わなかったとすれば、指紋の各線が一致しますから、あるいは後の指紋が先の指紋を隠してしまうこともできるでしょうが、そういうことはまずあり得ませんし、たとえそうだとしても、この場合結論は変らないのです。

　しかし、あの電燈を消したのが犯人だとすれば、スイッチにその指紋が残っていなければなりません。僕はもしや警察では君の指紋の線と線との間に残っている先の指紋を見落しているのではないかと思って、自分でしらべてみたのですが、少しもそんな痕跡がないのです。つまり、あのスイッチには、後にも先にも、君の指紋が捺されているだけなのです。——どうして古本屋の人達の指紋が残っていなかったのか、それはよく分りませんが、多分、あの部屋の電燈はつけっぱなしで、一度も消したことがないのでしょう。

　君、以上の事柄は一体何を語っているでしょう。僕はこういう風に考えるのですよ。一人の荒い棒縞の着物を着た男が、——その男は多分死んだ女の幼馴染で、失恋という理由なんかも考えら

The Case of the Murder on D Hill

and may have been motivated by this lost love, knew that the owner of the secondhand bookstore went out to sell at night markets and this man attacked the woman while he was out. She must have known this man well, because there is no evidence that she cried out or struggled. Then, having thoroughly completed his objective, the man turned off the electric light in order to delay the discovery of the corpse and walked away. However, the man's one mistake was that he didn't know that the lattice of the shoji was open, and that when he shut it in surprise, he was seen by two students who were in the storefront by chance. Then, once the man was outside, he suddenly realized that when he turned off the electric light he must have left fingerprints on the switch. These had to be erased no matter what. But it would be dangerous for him to sneak into the room again in the same way. But then a bright idea came to him. This idea was to be the one to discover the murder himself. By doing so, not only would he simply be able to eliminate himself from suspicion regarding the earlier fingerprints by turning on the light himself without seeming the slightest bit unnatural, but who would ever think that the person who discovered the crime would be the culprit himself? So it was doubly

★

■motivate 動 ～する動機を与える　■delay 動 ～を遅らせる　■by chance 偶然に　■sneak into ～に忍び込む　■eliminate 動 ～を除外する

れますね——古本屋の主人が夜店を出すことを知っていてその留守の間に女を襲うのです。声を立てたり抵抗したりした形跡がないのですから、女はその男をよく知っていたに相違ありません。で、まんまと目的を果した男は、死骸の発見を後らすために、電燈を消して立去ったのです。しかし、この男の一期(いちご)の不覚は、障子の格子のあいているのを知らなかったこと、そして、驚いてそれを閉めた時に、偶然店先にいた二人の学生に姿を見られたことでした。それから、男は一旦外へ出ましたが、ふと気がついたのは、電燈を消した時、スイッチに指紋が残ったに相違ないということです。これはどうしても消してしまわねばなりません。しかしもう一度同じ方法で部屋の中へ忍込むのは危険です。そこで、男は一つの妙案を思いつきました。それは、自から殺人事件の発見者になることです。そうすれば、少しも不自然もなく、自分の手で電燈をつけて、以前の指紋に対する疑をなくしてしまうことができるばかりでなく、まさか、発見者が犯人だろうとは誰しも考えませんからね、二重の利益があるのです。こうして、彼は何食わぬ顔で警察のやり方を見ていたのです。大胆にも証言さえしました。しかも、その結果は彼の思う壺だったのですよ。五日たっても十日たっても、誰も彼を捕えに来るものはなかったのですからね」

to his benefit, you see. In this way, he watched the police's methods with the appearance of innocence. In his audacity he even gave a statement. And the result was a bull's-eye, just as he imagined. Five, ten days on, still no one has come to arrest him."

With what expression did Akechi Kogoro listen to my story? I expected that he would make some sort of strange expression or cut me off as I spoke. But to my surprise, his face appeared expressionless. Although he was not ordinarily the kind to let his feelings show, he was far too calm. He had sat silently ruffling his hair from start to finish. Wondering just how shameless a man he could be, I proceeded to my final point.

"You are going to ask me, if that's true, then where did the culprit enter and how did he flee? Certainly, if that point cannot be clarified then knowing all the rest is to no avail. But unfortunately for you I've found this out as well. The result of the investigation that evening appeared to be that there was absolutely no trace of the culprit leaving. But seeing as there was a murder, there is no way that the culprit did not come and go somehow, so I could only think that something had been overlooked in the detectives' search. Although the police had taken

■audacity 名大胆さ　■bull's-eye 名大当たり　■cut ~ off ~の話をさえぎる
■flee 動逃げる　■clarify 動 ~を明らかにする　■to no avail (努力などが) 無駄に

この私の話を、明智小五郎はどんな表情で聴いていたか。私は、恐らく話の中途で、何か変った表情をするか、言葉を挟むだろうと予期していた。ところが、驚いたことには、彼の顔には何の表情も現れぬのだ。一体平素から心を色に現さぬたちではあったけれど、あまり平気すぎる。彼は始終例の髪の毛をモジャモジャやりながら、黙り込んでいるのだ。私は、どこまでずうずうしい男だろうと思いながら最後の点に話を進めた。

「君はきっと、それじゃ、その犯人はどこから入って、どこから逃げたかと反問するでしょう。確に、その点が明かにならなければ、他のすべてのことが分っても何の甲斐もないのですからね。だが、遺憾ながら、それも僕が探り出したのですよ。あの晩の捜査の結果では、全然犯人の出て行った形跡がないようにみえました。しかし、殺人があった以上、犯人が出入しなかったはずはないのですから、刑事の捜索にどこか抜目があったと考えるほかはありません。警察でもそれには随分苦心した様子ですが、不幸にして、彼等は、僕という一介の書生に及ばなかったのですよ。

considerable pains, unfortunately, they were no match for a mere student: me.

"Well, actually, it was a simple matter, you see. This is what I thought: first, the police had already questioned everyone thoroughly, so there was no reason to doubt the people of the neighborhood. That being the case, might the culprit not have taken his leave in a way that, even if he caught someone's attention, they would not realized that he was the culprit? Then if someone had witnessed him leaving, it would not be a problem, right? In other words, he might have made use of a blind spot in people's attentiveness—yes, just as there are blind spots in our vision, there are blind spots in our powers of attention, too—and hidden himself, just as a magician somehow hides a large object before the very eyes of his viewers. Then, I set my eyes on Asahiya, the soba store two doors down from the secondhand bookstore."

The watchmaker and the confectioner's stood to the right of the bookstore, and to the left stood a *tabi* store and the soba store.

"I went there and asked them if a man had asked to use the facilities at around eight o'clock on the night of the incident. I am sure you are familiar with Asahiya yourself,

■take one's leave 立ち去る　■blind spot 盲点　■attentiveness 图注意力
■confectioner 图菓子屋　■facility 图トイレ

ナアニ、実は下らぬ事なんですがね、僕はこう思ったのです。これほど警察が取調べているのだから、近所の人達に疑うべき点は先ずあるまい。もしそうだとすれば、犯人は、何か、人の目にふれても、それが犯人だとは気づかれぬような方法で通ったのじゃないだろうか、そして、それを目撃した人はあっても、まるで問題にしなかったのではなかろうか、とね。つまり、人間の注意力の盲点——我々の目に盲点があると同じように、注意力にもそれがありますよ——を利用して、手品使が見物の目の前で、大きな品物をわけもなく隠すように、自分自身を隠したのかも知れませんからね。そこで、僕が目をつけたのは、あの古本屋の一軒おいて隣の旭屋という蕎麦屋です」

　古本屋の右へ時計屋、菓子屋と並び、左へ足袋屋、蕎麦屋と並んでいるのだ。

「僕はあすこへ行って、事件の当夜八時頃に、便所を借りて行った男はないかと聞いてみたのです。あの旭屋は君も知っているでしょうが、店から土間続きで、裏木戸まで行けるようになってい

The Case of the Murder on D Hill

but the dirt floor there extends from the shop to a back door, and the facilities are just outside the back door, so if one uses the lavatory there, they must go out the back door and come back in again. Because the ice cream man has his store at the corner where the alley comes out, there is no way he would see. And because it is a soba restaurant, it is the most natural thing to ask to use the lavatory. Upon asking, I heard that on that evening the lady of the house was out and only the owner was in the store, making it ideal. What a splendid idea, don't you think?

"Sure enough, there was a customer who had used the lavatory at precisely the hour and minute in question. But, unfortunately, the owner of Asahiya could not remember the man's face or whether he was wearing a striped kimono. I immediately passed this on to Detective Kobayashi through my friend. The detective went and investigated the soba place himself, but he found out nothing further."

I paused slightly to give Akechi room to respond. In this position, he could not possibly fail to say something this time. However, he just kept running his fingers through his hair as always while looking on with an air of superiority. Until this point I had been using indirect

★
■lavatory 名お手洗い　■ideal 名理想（的な状態）　■give ~ room to 〜に…する ゆとりを与える　■superiority 名優越、優位　■indirect method 間接法

て、その裏木戸のすぐ側に便所があるのですから、便所を借りるようにみせかけて、裏口から出て行って、また入って来るのはわけはありませんからね。——例のアイスクリーム屋は路地を出た角に店を出していたのですから、見つかるはずはありません——それに、相手が蕎麦屋ですから、便所を借りるということがきわめて自然なんです。聞けば、あの晩はおかみさんは不在で、主人だけが店の間にいたそうですから、おあつらえ向きなんです。君、なんとすてきな、思いつきではありませんか。

　そして、案の定、ちょうどその時分に便所を借りた客があったのです。ただ、残念なことには、旭屋の主人は、その男の顔形とか着物の縞柄なぞを少しも覚えていないのですがね。——僕は早速この事を例の友達を通じて、小林刑事に知らせてやりましたよ。刑事は自分でも蕎麦屋を調べたようでしたが、それ以上何も分らなかったのです——」

　私は少し言葉を切って、明智に発言の余裕を与えた。彼の立場は、この際何とか一言いわないでいられぬはずだ。ところが、彼は相変らず頭を掻まわしながら、すまし込んでいるのだ。私はこれまで、敬意を表する意味で間接法を用いていたのを直接法に改めねばならなかった。

The Case of the Murder on D Hill

methods out of respect for him, but now I had to change to more direct methods.

"Look, Akechi, you know what I'm getting at here. Irrefutable evidence is pointing at you. I confess, from the bottom of my heart, that I somehow cannot bring myself to doubt you, but when all the evidence is put together like this, I don't see what other solution there is.... I wondered if one of the people in those row houses had a *yukata* with bold stripes, and I took great pains to investigate, but no one did. That is believable. Even if someone did have the same striped *yukata*, it's rare to wear clothes that flashy. Besides, the trick with the fingerprints and the trick with using the conveniences were really clever—these are tricks that could not be imitated in the slightest by someone who wasn't a crime scholar like yourself. And then, the strangest thing was, although you've said that the deceased was a childhood friend of yours, that night, when they were looking into the wife's background, you were listening and you did not state this at all, did you?

"Now, the only thing you have left to rely upon is whether or not you have an alibi. But that is useless too. Do you remember, on our way home that night,

★

■direct method 直接法　■irrefutable 形反論の余地がない　■bring oneself to 〜する気になる　■take great pains to 〜するのに大いに骨を折る　■flashy 形派手な　■alibi 名アリバイ、現場不在証明

「君、明智君、僕のいう意味が分るでしょう。動かぬ証拠が君を指さしているのですよ。白状すると、僕はまだ心の底では、どうしても君を疑う気になれないのですが、こういう風に証拠が揃っていては、どうも仕方がありません。……僕は、もしやあの長屋の内に、太い棒縞の浴衣を持っている人がないかと思って、随分骨を折って調べてみましたが、一人もありません。それももっともですよ。同じ棒縞の浴衣でも、あの格子に一致するような派手なのを着る人は珍しいのですからね。それに、指紋のトリックにしても、便所を借りるというトリックにしても、実に巧妙で、君のような犯罪学者でなければ、ちょっと真似のできない芸当ですよ。それから、第一おかしいのは、君はあの死人の細君と幼馴染だといっていながら、あの晩、細君の身許調べなんかあった時に、側で聞いていて、少しもそれを申立てなかったではありませんか。

さて、そうなると唯一の頼みはAlibiの有無です。ところが、それも駄目なんです。君は覚えていますか、あの晩帰り途で、白梅軒へ来るまで君がどこにいたかということを、僕は聞きましたね。

how I asked you where you had been before coming to the White Plum Blossom Café? You answered that you had been strolling around the area for about an hour. If someone had seen you out for a walk, it would've been a natural thing to stop during your walk and use the conveniences at the soba place, wouldn't it? Is what I've said mistaken, Akechi? How about it? If possible may I hear your explanation?"

Dear readers, what do you think that odd fellow Akechi Kogoro did when I finished speaking? Do you think he may have prostrated himself in shame? Why on earth I do not know, but I was taken aback by his completely unexpected reaction. Which is to say, he suddenly guffawed.

"Oh, how rude of me, how rude. I certainly do not mean to laugh at you, but you just looked so serious," Akechi said by way of defense. "Your ideas are quite interesting. I am delighted to have found a friend like you. But regrettably, your reasoning is a bit superficial and materialist. Take this for an example. As concerns my relationship with that woman, did you attempt a probing, psychological investigation into what sort of childhood friends we were? Or into whether I had a

■prostrate oneself ひれ伏す　■guffaw 動ゲラゲラと笑う　■regrettably 副残念ながら　■superficial 形外面的な　■materialist 名物質主義者

君は一時間ほど、その辺を散歩していたと答えたでしょう。たとえ、君の散歩姿を見た人があったとしても、散歩の途中で、蕎麦屋の便所を借りるなどはあり勝ちのことですからね。明智君、僕のいうことが間違っていますか。どうです。もしできるなら君の弁明を聞こうじゃありませんか」

　読者諸君、私がこういって詰めよった時、奇人明智小五郎は何をしたと思います。面目なさに俯伏してしまったとでも思うのですか。どうしてどうして、彼はまるで意表外のやり方で、私の荒胆をひしいだのです。というのは、彼はいきなりゲラゲラと笑い出したのです。

「いや失敬失敬、決して笑うつもりではなかったのですけれど、君はあまり真面目だもんだから」明智は弁解するようにいった。「君の考えはなかなか面白いですよ。僕は君のような友達をみつけたことを嬉しく思いますよ。しかし、惜しいことには、君の推理はあまりに外面的で、そして物質的ですよ。例えばですね。僕とあの女との関係についても、君は、僕達がどんな風な幼馴染だったかということを、内面的に心理的に調べてみましたか。僕が以前あの女と恋愛関係があったかどうか。また現に彼女を恨んでいるかどうか。君にはそれくらいのことが推察できなかったのです

The Case of the Murder on D Hill

romantic relationship with that woman previously? Or indeed whether I held a grudge against her? Couldn't you even figure those things out? As for why I did not say on that night that I knew her, the reason is simple. I did not know anything which would be useful as reference. We had already parted ways before we had even entered elementary school. Although recently, by chance, I had learned it was her and we had spoken two or three times."

"Then what, for instance, should one think about the fingerprints?"

"Do you think I have done nothing since that evening? I have done quite a bit with the case myself. I wander around D Hill nearly every day. In particular I went to the secondhand bookstore quite a lot. I cornered the proprietor and probed into all sorts of matters. I confided in him then that I had known his wife, but that was actually to my advantage. Just as you learned of the state of the police investigation through a reporter, I got information about it from the proprietor of the secondhand bookstore. I also soon learned about the fingerprints of which you speak, and thinking it was strange myself I made some investigations, but, ha ha.... It's a funny story. The wires in the light bulb

■reference 图参考　■wander around うろうろ歩き回る　■proprietor 图店主
■confide in ～に秘密などを打ち明ける

か。あの晩、なぜ彼女を知っていることをいわなかったか、そのわけは簡単ですよ。僕は何も参考になるような事柄を知らなかったのです。僕は、まだ小学校へも入らぬ時分に彼女と分れた切りなのですからね。もっとも、最近偶然そのことが分って、二三度話し合ったことはありますけれど」

「では、例えば指紋のことはどういう風に考えたらいいのですか？」
「君は、僕があれから何もしないでいたと思うのですか。僕もこれでなかなかやったのですよ。D坂は毎日のようにうろついていましたよ。ことに古本屋へはよく行きました。そして主人をつかまえて色々探ったのです。——細君を知っていたことはその時打明けたのですが、それがかえって便宜になりましたよ——君が新聞記者を通じて警察の模様を知ったように、僕はあの古本屋の主人から、それを聞出していたんです。今の指紋のことも、じきに分りましたから、僕も妙に思ってしらべてみたのですが、ハハ……、笑い話ですよ。電球の線が切れていたのです。誰も消しやしなかったのですよ。僕がスイッチをひねったために燈がついたと思ったのは間違で、あの時、慌てて電燈を動かしたので、一度切れたタングステンが、つながったのですよ。スイッチに僕の指紋だけしかなかったのは、当りまえなのです。あの晩、君は障子の

The Case of the Murder on D Hill

had disconnected. Nobody turned it off at all. It was my mistake to think that the light came on because I twisted the switch; when I did so, in my panic I jostled the light, and so the previously disconnected tungsten reconnected then. It is perfectly natural, then, that only my fingerprints were found on the switch. You told me that evening that you had seen the light on through the gaps in the shoji. If that is so, then the light bulb must have gotten disconnected after that. Those old light bulbs do sometimes break on their own, without anyone doing anything, you know. Now, then, as for the color of the culprit's kimono, rather than explain that myself...."

Saying that, he began to dig here and there in the mountains of books that surrounded him, until eventually he dug out one old, worn Western book.

"Have you ever read this? It's a book called *On the Witness Stand* by Munsterberg. Please take a look at just these ten lines at the beginning of this chapter called 'Illusions.'"

As I listened to his confident reasoning, I became gradually aware of my own failure. I took the book from him and read, just as I had been told. What was written there was roughly as follows.

■disconnect 動 切断する　■jostle 動 (乱暴に) 押す　■tungsten 图 タングステン《金属元素のひとつ》　■reconnect 動 〜を再びつなぐ　■dig out 掘り出す

すき間から電燈のついているのを見たといいましたね。とすれば、電球の切れたのは、その後ですよ。古い電球は、どうもしないでも、独りでに切れることがありますからね。それから、犯人の着物の色のことですが、これは僕が説明するよりも……」

　彼はそういって、彼の身辺の書物の山を、あちらこちら発掘していたが、やがて、一冊の古ぼけた洋書を掘りだして来た。

「君、これを読んだことがありますか、ミュンスターベルヒの『心理学と犯罪』という本ですが、この『錯覚』という章の冒頭を十行ばかり読んでごらんなさい」

　私は、彼の自信ありげな議論を聞いている内に、段々私自身の失敗を意識し始めていた。で、いわれるままにその書物を受取って、読んでみた。そこには大体次のようなことが書いてあった。

The Case of the Murder on D Hill

There had been an automobile accident. Before the court, one of the witnesses who had sworn to tell "the whole truth, and nothing but the truth," declared that the entire road was dry and dusty; the other swore that it had rained and the road was muddy. The one said that the automobile was running very slowly; the other, that he had never seen an automobile rushing more rapidly. The first swore that there were only two or three people on the village road; the other, that a large number of men, women, and children were passing by. Both witnesses were highly respectable gentlemen, neither of whom had the slightest interest in changing the facts as he remembered them.

Akechi waited for me to finish reading this, and then as he turned the pages again he spoke.

"That was something which actually occurred. Now, there's this chapter called 'The Memory of the Witness.' Nearly halfway through there is a story of an experiment which was planned in advance. It does involve the color of clothing, so please give it a read although it may be bothersome to do so."

It was the following account.

■swear to ～することを誓う　■turn a page ページをめくる　■in advance あらかじめ　■bothersome 形 面倒な

かつて一つの自動車犯罪事件があった。法廷において、真実を申立てるむね宣誓した証人の一人は、問題の道路は全然乾燥してほこり立っていたと主張し、いま一人の証人は、雨降りの挙句で、道路はぬかるんでいたと誓言した。一人は、問題の自動車は徐行していたともいい、他の一人は、あのように早く走っている自動車を見たことがないと述べた。また前者は、その村道には二三人しかいなかったといい、後者は、男や女や子供の通行人が沢山あったと陳述した。この両人の証人は、共に尊敬すべき紳士で、事実を曲弁したとて、何の利益があるはずもない人々だった。

　私がそれを読み終るのを待って明智はさらに本のページを繰りながらいった。
　「これは実際あったことですが、今度は、この『証人の記憶』という章があるでしょう。その中ほどの所に、あらかじめ計画して実験した話があるのですよ。ちょうど着物の色のことが出てますから、面倒でしょうが、まあちょっと読んでごらんなさい」

　それは左のような記事であった。

The Case of the Murder on D Hill

[...] There was, for instance, two years ago [the book was published in 1911] in Göttingen a meeting of a scientific association, made up of jurists, psychologists, and physicians, all, therefore, men well trained in careful observation. Somewhere in the same street there was that evening a public festivity of the carnival. Suddenly, in the midst of the scholarly meeting, the doors open, a clown in highly colored costume rushes in in mad excitement, and a Negro with a revolver in hand follows him. In the middle of the hall first the one, then the other, shouts wild phrases; then the one falls to the ground, the other jumps on him; then a shot, and suddenly both are out of the room. The whole affair took less than twenty seconds. All were completely taken by surprise, and no one, with the exception of the President, had the slightest idea that every word and action had been rehearsed beforehand, or that photographs had been taken of the scene. It seemed most natural that the President should beg the members to write down individually an exact report, inasmuch as he felt sure that the matter would come before the courts. *(I have omitted a passage here reporting that their memories were full of mistakes and giving percentages.)* Only four persons, for

■jurist 名法学者 ■clown 名道化師 ■Negro 名黒人《差別的表現》 ■revolver 名リボルバー、回転式拳銃 ■beg ~ to ~に…してほしいと頼む ■inasmuch as ~のために

（前略）一例を上げるならば、一昨年（この書物の出版は一九一一年）ゲッティンゲンにおいて、法律家、心理学者および物理学者よりなる、ある学術上の集会が催されたことがある。したがって、そこに集ったのは、皆、綿密な観察に熟練した人達ばかりであった。その町には、あたかもカーニバルのお祭騒ぎが演じられていたが、突然、この学究的な会合の最中に、戸が開かれてけばけばしい衣裳をつけた一人の道化が、狂気のように飛び込んで来た。見ると、その後から一人の黒人が手にピストルを持って追駆けて来るのだ。ホールの真中で、彼等はかたみがわりに、恐ろしい言葉をどなり合ったが、やがて道化の方がバッタリ床に倒れると、黒人はその上に躍りかかった。そして、ポンとピストルの音がした。と、たちまち彼等は二人共、かき消すように室を出て行ってしまった。全体の出来事が二十秒とはかからなかった。人々は無論非常に驚かされた。座長のほかには、誰一人、それらの言葉や動作が、あらかじめ予習されていたこと、その光景が写真に撮られたことなどを悟ったものはなかった。で、座長が、これはいずれ法廷に持出される問題だからというので、会員各自に正確な記録を書くことを頼んだのは、ごく自然にみえた。（中略、この間に、彼等の記録がいかに間違にみちていたかを、パーセンテージを示して記してある）黒人が頭に何もかぶっていなかったことをいい当てたのは、四十人の内でたった四人きりで、ほかの人達は山高帽子をかぶっていたと書いたものもあれば、シルクハットだったと書くものもあるという有様だっ

instance, among forty noticed that the Negro had nothing on his head; the others gave him a derby, or a high hat, and so on. In addition to this, a red suit, a brown one, a striped one, a coffee-colored jacket, shirt sleeves, and similar costumes were invented for him. He wore in reality white trousers and a black jacket with a large red necktie. [...]

"As Munsterberg shrewdly observed," Akechi began, "people's observations and memories are not to be relied upon. Even the scholars in this example were not able to tell apart the colors of his clothing. Do I think it is impossible that those students mistook the kimono's color that night? They may have seen someone. But that person was not wearing a striped kimono. Of course, it was not me. The observation you hit upon about the striped *yukata* seen through the gaps in the lattice is rather interesting in and of itself, but is it not a little too perfect? Could you not at least believe in my innocence rather than such a concurrence of coincidences? Then, finally, we come to the man who asked to use the soba seller's lavatory. On this point I had the same idea as you. Try as I might, I thought of no other route for the

★

■derby 図山高帽子　■shrewdly 図抜け目なく　■tell apart　見分ける　■hit upon　思いつく　■concurrence 図符号、一致

た。着物についても、ある者は赤だといい、あるものは茶色だといい、ある者は縞だといい、あるものはコーヒ色だといい、そのほか種々様々の色合が彼のために説明せられた。ところが、黒人は実際は、白ズボンに黒の上衣を着て、大きな赤のネクタイを結んでいたのだ。(後略)

「ミュンスターベルヒが賢くも説破した通り」と明智は始めた。「人間の観察や人間の記憶なんて、実にたよりないものですよ。この例にあるような学者達でさえ、服の色の見分がつかなかったのです。私が、あの晩の学生達は着物の色を見違えたと考えるのが無理でしょうか。彼等は何者かを見たかもしれません。しかしその者は棒縞の着物なんか着ていなかったはずです。無論僕ではなかったのです。格子のすき間から、棒縞の浴衣を思付いた君の着眼は、なかなか面白いには面白いですが、あまりあつらえむきすぎるじゃありませんか。少くとも、そんな偶然の符合を信ずるよりは、君は、僕の潔白を信じてくれるわけにはいかぬでしょうか。さて最後に、蕎麦屋の便所を借りた男のことですがね。この点は僕も君と同じ考だったのです。どうも、あの旭屋のほかに犯人の通路はないと思ったのですよ。で僕もあすこへ行って調べてみましたが、その結果は、残念ながら、君と正反対の結論に達したのです。実際は便所を借りた男なんてなかったのですよ」

culprit to take but through Asahiya. So I also went there and investigated, but the result was, unfortunately, that I reached the opposite conclusion from you. In fact, there was no man who used the lavatory."

As the reader has likely already noticed, Akechi had thus repudiated the testimony of the witnesses, the culprit's fingerprints, and even the culprit's passageway in an attempt to prove his own innocence, but at the same time, was he not repudiating the crime itself? I did not have the slightest idea what he was thinking.

"Then, you have an idea of who the culprit is?"

"I do," he answered, ruffling his hair. "My approach is a little different from yours. Physical evidence and so on all depends on how you interpret it. The best method of detection is to see into the human mind psychologically. But this is a matter of the detective's own ability. Anyway, I tried to put the emphasis in that direction this time.

"The first thing that attracted my attention was the fact that there were fresh wounds on the body of the bookseller's wife. Shortly thereafter, I heard that there were similar wounds on the body of the soba man's wife. I'm sure you know this as well. However, these women's husbands did not seem like that sort of violent man. Both

■repudiated 斃 〜を否定する　■put the emphasis 重きをおく

読者もすでに気づかれたであろうが、明智はこうして、証人の申立てを否定し、犯人の指紋を否定し、犯人の通路をさえ否定して、自分の無罪を証拠立てようとしているが、しかしそれは同時に、犯罪そのものを否定することになりはしないか。私は彼が何を考えているのか少しも分らなかった。

「で、君は犯人の見当がついているのですか」
「ついていますよ」彼は頭をモジャモジャやりながら答えた。「僕のやり方は、君とは少し違うのです。物質的な証拠なんてものは、解釈の仕方でどうでもなるものですよ。一番いい探偵法は、心理的に人の心の奥底を見抜くことです。だが、これは探偵者自身の能力の問題ですがね。ともかく、僕は今度はそういう方面に重きをおいてやってみましたよ。
　最初僕の注意をひいたのは、古本屋の細君の身体中にある生傷のあったことです。それから間もなく、僕は蕎麦屋の細君の身体にも同じような生傷があることを聞込みました。これは君も知っているでしょう。しかし、彼女等の夫は、そんな乱暴者でもなさそうです。古本屋にしても蕎麦屋にしても、おとなしそうな、物分りのいい男なんですからね。僕は何となく、そこにある秘密が伏在

The Case of the Murder on D Hill

the bookseller and the soba man are unassuming, sensible men, as you know. Somehow, I could not help but suspect there was some secret concealed there. So first I collared the bookseller to try to get the secret out from his own lips. Because I said that I had been an acquaintance of his dead wife, this put him somewhat at ease and it went relatively easily. Then, I was able to get a certain strange fact out of him. However, next was the proprietor of the soba place, and he is, despite appearances, a rather strong-headed man, so it required some hard work to get anything out of him. But by means of a certain process I was highly successful.

"I'm sure you know that the psychological associative approach to diagnosis has begun to be used in criminal investigations as well. It is a method by which lots of simple trigger words are given and the speed at which the suspect forms associations is measured. However, I am not necessarily limited to saying simple trigger words such as 'dog,' 'house,' or 'river,' as psychologists are, nor do I believe there is always a need for the help of a chronoscope. For one who has the knack of it, such formalities are not especially needed. As proof of that, didn't the people of old who were called great judges

★

■unassuming 形控えめな ■concealed 形隠れた ■collar 動〜を引き止める
■strong-headed 形断固とした ■diagnosis 名診断 ■trigger word 刺激語
■chronoscope 名クロノスコープ《速度を測定する装置》 ■knack 名こつ

しているのではないかと疑わないではいられなかったのです。で、僕はまず古本屋の主人を捉えて、彼の口からその秘密を探り出そうとしました。僕が死んだ細君の知合だというので、彼もいくらか気を許していましたから、それは比較的楽に行きました。そして、ある変な事実を聞出すことができたのです。ところが、今度は蕎麦屋の主人ですが、彼は、ああ見えてもなかなかしっかりした男ですから、探り出すのにかなり骨が折れましたよ。でも、僕はある方法によって、うまく成功したのです。

　君は、心理学上の聯想診断法が、犯罪捜査の方面にも利用され始めたのを知っているでしょう。沢山の簡単な刺戟語を与えて、それに対する嫌疑者の観念聯合の遅速を計る、あの方法です。しかし、あれは必ずしも、心理学者のいうように、犬だとか家だとか川だとか、簡単な刺戟語には限らないし、そしてまた、常にクロノスコープの助けを借りる必要もないと、僕は思いますよ。聯想診断のこつを悟ったものにとっては、そのような形式は大した必要ではないのです。それが証拠に、昔の名判官とか名探偵とかいわれる人は心理学が今日のように発達しない以前から、ただ彼等の天稟によって、知らずしらずの間に、この心理的方法を実行していたではありませんか。大岡越前守なども確かにその一人で

The Case of the Murder on D Hill

or detectives unknowingly practice these psychological methods using only their natural talents, long before psychology had developed to the state it is in today? Ooka, the Governor of Echizen, was certainly one such person. Or to speak of novels, there is a part at the beginning of Poe's *The Murders in the Rue Morgue* where Dupin correctly guesses what is on his friend's mind from one single movement of his body, does he not? Doyle mimics this—in *The Adventure of the Resident Patient*, Holmes makes his usual reasoning, but they are all associative diagnoses of a sort. The variety of mechanical methods of psychologists are simply made for ordinary men without these gifts of insight. I have digressed slightly, but in this sense, I used associative techniques of a sort with the soba man. I devised a number of traps for him in our conversation, and a very dull chat it was, too. And then I studied his psychological reaction. But as this was an extremely delicate psychological problem, as well as a rather complex one, I shall save the details for when we speak at leisure. At any rate, as a result I reached a conclusion. In other words, I found the culprit.

"However, I don't have a single piece of physical evidence. Therefore I cannot take it to the police. Even if I went to them, I doubt they would listen. Besides, I

■Dupin 图デュパン《ポーの推理小説に登場する名探偵》　■mimic 動真似る　■gift 图特別な才能　■digress 動本題からそれる　■dull 形つまらない　■at leisure　ゆっくりと

すよ。小説でいえば、ポオの『ル・モルグ』の始めに、デュパンが友達の身体の動き方一つによって、その心に思っていることをいい当てる所がありますね。ドイルもそれを真似て、『レジデント・ペーシェント』の中で、ホームズに同じような推理をやらせますが、これらは皆、ある意味の聯想診断ですからね。心理学者の種々の機械的方法は、ただこうした天稟の洞察力を持たぬ凡人のために作られたものに過ぎませんよ。話がわきみちに入りましたが、僕はそういう意味で、蕎麦屋の主人に対して、一種の聯想診断をやったのです。僕は彼に色々の話をしかけました。それもごくつまらない世間話をね。そして、彼の心理的反応を研究したのです。しかし、これは非常にデリケートな心持の問題で、それにかなり複雑してますから、詳しいことはいずれゆっくり話すとして、ともかくその結果、僕は一つの確信に到達しました。つまり犯人をみつけたのです。

　しかし物質的な証拠というものは一つもないのです。だから、警察に訴えるわけにも行きません。よし訴えても、恐らく取上げてくれないでしょう。それに、僕が犯人を知りながら、手をつかね

The Case of the Murder on D Hill

have another reason for folding my arms and watching, despite knowing who the culprit is, and that is because the criminal did not have the slightest bit of malice. It is a strange way to put it, but this murder was carried out on the agreement of the culprit and the victim. No, perhaps you could say it was carried out according to the victim's wishes."

I turned various ideas over in my mind, but I was unable to understand what he was thinking at all. I forgot to be ashamed of my own failure and bent my ear to listen to his fantastic reasoning.

"So, if I may tell you my idea, the murderer is the proprietor of Asahiya. He told the story about the man using the lavatory in order to hide his crime. But no, that was not his invention in the least. We are the ones to blame. Both you and I asked him whether there had been such a man, and this was like instigating him. On top of this, he must have mistaken us for detectives or the like. Now, as for why he committed the murder.... I feel that this case has allowed me to see some of the most surprising and pathetic secrets that are hidden behind the façade of this world, which is seemingly so very innocent. This is, indeed, the type of thing which can only be found in the world of nightmares.

❖

■fold one's arms 腕をこまねく ■malice 名 悪意 ■bend one's ear to listen to 〜に耳を傾ける ■instigate 動 〜を教唆する ■pathetic 形 陰惨な ■façade 名 うわべ《フランス語》

てみているもう一つの理由は、この犯罪には少しも悪意がなかったという点です。変な言い方ですが、この殺人事件は、犯人と被害者と同意の上で行われたのです。いや、ひょっとしたら被害者自身の希望によって行われたのかもしれません」

　私は色々想像をめぐらしてみたけれど、どうにも彼の考えていることが分りかねた。私自身の失敗を恥じることを忘れて、彼のこの奇怪な推理に耳を傾けた。

「で、僕の考えをいいますとね、殺人者は旭屋の主人なのです。彼は罪跡をくらますためにあんな便所を借りた男のことをいったのですよ。いや、しかしそれは何も彼の創案でも何でもない。我々が悪いのです。君にしろ僕にしろ、そういう男がなかったかと、こちらから問を構えて、彼を教唆したようなものですからね。それに、彼は僕達を刑事かなんかと思違えていたのです。では、彼は何故に殺人罪を犯したか。……僕はこの事件によって、うわべはきわめて何気なさそうな、この人世の裏面に、どんなに意外な、陰惨な秘密が隠されているかということを、まざまざと見せつけられたような気がします。それは、実に、あの悪夢の世界でしか見出すことのできないような種類のものだったのです。

"The proprietor of Asahiya has followed in the footsteps of the Marquis de Sade and is a terrible sadist, and what a twist of fate to discover two doors down a woman Masoch. The bookseller's wife was equal to him in her masochism. So, with the cleverness specific to their particular sickness, they committed adultery without being found out by anyone.... You see now what I meant by this being a murder by consent.... Until recently the abnormal desires of each had just barely been met by their legitimate spouse. That the bookseller's wife and the man from Asahiya's wife had the same sort of wounds is proof of that. But it need hardly be said that this did not satisfy them. So when they found the person they had each been searching for right under their nose, it is not difficult to imagine that they came to a very quick understanding with each other, is it? But the result was more than a trick of fate. Due to their synthesis of passive and active forces, their disgraceful behavior started building in intensity. And finally, on that night, it was the cause of an incident they certainly never had hoped for...."

I shuddered involuntarily as I heard Akechi's bizarre conclusion. What a strange case this one was!

★

■Marquis de Sade マルキ・ド・サド《フランスの貴族、作家》 ■by consent 合意の上で ■legitimate spouse 正当な配偶者 ■right under one's nose 目と鼻の先に ■synthesis 図合成 ■involuntarily 副思わず

旭屋の主人というのは、サード卿の流れをくんだ、ひどい惨虐色情者で、何という運命のいたずらでしょう、一軒おいて隣に、女のマゾッホを発見したのです。古本屋の細君は彼に劣らぬ被虐色情者だったのです。そして、彼等は、そういう病者に特有の巧みさをもって、誰にもみつけられずに、姦通していたのです。……君、僕が合意の殺人だといった意味が分るでしょう。……彼等は、最近までは、各々、正当の夫や妻によって、その病的な欲望を、かろうじてみたしていました。古本屋の細君にも、旭屋の細君にも、同じような生傷のあったのはその証拠です。しかし、彼等がそれに満足しなかったのはいうまでもありません。ですから目と鼻の近所に、お互の探し求めている人間を発見した時、彼等の間に非常に敏速な了解の成立したことは想像に難くないではありませんか。ところがその結果は、運命のいたずらが過ぎたのです。彼等の、パッシヴとアクティヴの力の合成によって、狂態が漸次倍加されて行きました。そして、遂にあの夜、この、彼等とても決して願わなかった事件をひきおこしてしまったわけなのです……」

　私は、明智のこの異様な結論を聞いて、思わず身震いした。これはまあ、何という事件だ！

The Case of the Murder on D Hill

Just then, the mistress of the tobacconist downstairs brought up the evening paper. Akechi accepted it and took a look at the local news page, and before long, he sighed gently.

"Oh, it looks like he couldn't take it anymore and gave himself up. What a strange coincidence, to receive news like this just when we were talking about it."

I looked at where he was pointing. There, with a small headline and just ten lines of text, it was noted that the proprietor of Asahiya had turned himself in.

そこへ、下の煙草屋のおかみさんが、夕刊を持って来た。明智はこれを受取って、社会面を見ていたが、やがて、そっと溜息をついていった。

「アア、とうとう耐え切れなくなったとみえて、自首しましたよ。妙な偶然ですね。ちょうどその事を話していた時に、こんな報導に接するとは」

私は彼の指さす所を見た。そこには、小さい見出しで、十行ばかり、蕎麦屋の主人の自首したむねが記されてあった。

■turn oneself in 自首する

D坂の殺人事件

確かな読解のための英語表現［文法］

would + have

英文法のことを忘れてしまっていても、単語さえわかれば英文の意味をある程度理解することはできます。ただし、文法がわかれば、英語の細かいニュアンスを把握できて、英文を読むのがぐんと楽しくなります。学校で習ったことを少し復習してみましょう。ここでは、willの過去形、wouldにhaveがついたかたちを扱います。

> And since I have always had a small appetite and little in my purse, I would have two or three cups of cheap coffee and take an hour or two over them. （p.80, 下から6行目）
> それも、元来食欲の少い方なので、一つは囊中(のうちゅう)の乏しいせいもあってだが、安いコーヒーを二杯も三杯もお代りして、一時間も二時間もじっとしているのだ。

【解説】このwould haveは、過去の習慣を表すwould＋述語動詞のhave（「食べる、飲む」の意味）で構成されています。ここでwouldは「よく〜したものだ」という意味で、過去の習慣を表します。used toも似たような意味ですが、wouldのほうが、懐かしさなど、何らかの主観的な気持ちを込めて当時を思い起こす時に使われます。ここでは「あんな事件もあった」との思いを込めて語っているため、wouldを用いています。

> These sliding doors were of the type which specialists refer to as *muso*, meaning that the central portion which normally <u>would have</u> paper pasted over it was instead made into a narrow, vertical double lattice which could be opened and closed. （p.84, 下から9行目）
> その障子は、専門家の方では無窓(むそう)と称するもので、普通、紙をはるべき中央の部分が、こまかい縦の二重の格子になっていて、それが開閉できるのだ。

【解説】このwould haveは仮定法過去完了です。if節のない仮定法で、normallyが「通常ならば」という仮定の意味を表しています。which normally would have paper pasted over itは、直訳すると「通常だったならば、その上に紙が張られていたであろう」となります。

> In the first place, there was nowhere for my host and me to sit, and any careless movement <u>would have</u> sent the books tumbling down at once, possibly crushing us. （p.134, 下から7行目）
> 第一、主客二人の座る所もない、うっかり身動きしようものなら、たちまち本の土手くずれで、おしつぶされてしまうかも知れない。

【解説】同じくif節のない仮定法です。any careless movementの主語が「不注意な動きがあれば」の仮定の意味を表しています。would have sent the books tumbling down at onceは「あっというまに本が崩れてしまったかもしれない」となります。

> At a guess I <u>would have</u> said he was a student, but he <u>would have</u> made an exceptionally strange one.（p.136, 10行目）
> しいていえば書生であろうか、だが、書生にしてはよほど風変りな書生だ。

【解説】この文はwould haveが2か所出てきますが、いずれもif節のない仮定法です。1文目はat a guess「一目見れば」が仮定の意味で、それに仮定法過去完了のI would have saidが続き「私は言ったであろう」が直訳となります。butの後のwould have madeは、その前のhe was a studentを受けており「(書生だったとすれば)彼は非常に変わった書生であろう」です。

> it seemed that it <u>would have</u> been a little difficult to escape that way.（p.116, 8行目）
> ここから逃げるのはちょっと難しいように思われる。

【解説】このwould haveは、主節のseemedを受けて、時制の一致によりwillがwouldになったもので、it will have been a little difficult to escape that way. が元の形、すなわち未来完了形です。「その道を避けるというのはちょっと難しかっただろう」となります。

　この文を読み難くしている要因はこれだけではなく、itの連続にもあります。最初のitは形式主語で、that節が真主語です。さらに、thatの次のitも形式主語で、不定詞句のto escape that way「その道を避けるのは」が真主語です。

> Not only that, but were it an ape or something similar, there was no way it would not have left footprints and it would have also attracted people's attention.
> （p.128, 下から7行目）
>
> のみならず、猿類などだったら、足跡の残らぬはずはなく、また人目にもついたはずだ。

【解説】この文にも２つのwould haveがあり、andで結ばれています。were it an ape〜, という仮定法（ただし倒置）の条件節に続いて出てくるので、１つ目のwould haveはすぐに仮定法過去完了と見分けられるでしょう。andの後に出てくる２つ目も、同じ条件節からのつながりです。１つ目はnotが入って否定文（would not have left footprints「足跡が残っていないことはなかっただろう」）、２つ目は肯定文（would have attracted people's attention「人目を引いただろう」）と、分けて考えるのがポイントです。

> Had a snake wound itself around her neck, it would not have left that kind of mark. （p.128, 下から3行目）
>
> 蛇がまきついたとて、あんなあとは残らぬ。

【解説】同じく、前にHad a snake wound itselfという仮定法（倒置）の条件節があるので仮定法過去完了とわかります。ただし条件節に、譲歩のevenの意味が含まれているのがカギです。（Even）if a snake had wound 〜「蛇が〜としても」とevenを補って読めれば、「そんな種類の痕は残らなかっただろうに」と文脈が通ります。thoughやifの前に、このようにevenを補って読むことがあることを覚えておきましょう。

The Psychological Examination

心理試験

The Psychological Examination

I

Why Seiichiro Fukiya conceived of the terrible wickedness I record herein, what precisely motivated him, is unknown to me. Even if this were not the case, such matters would have little connection to this story. Observing the circumstances against which he struggled while studying at a certain university, one might suppose that he was pressed by his school fees. As a student of rare genius and unusual dedication, it is true that he lamented the fact that the extent to which he could read and think as he pleased was limited by the need to spend time on trivial piecework to pay his expenses. But would anyone commit such a great crime for so trivial a reason? Perhaps he was a congenital evildoer. Perhaps, indeed, he had uncontrollable desires of many sorts, not only for money to pay his school expenses. In any case, half a year had passed since the idea occurred to him. After endless deliberation and uncertainty over those long months, he had finally arrived at the decision to do the old woman in.

■conceive of 〜を思い立つ　■dedication 名熱心さ　■congenital 形先天的な　■evildoer 名悪人　■do〜in 〜を殺す

一

　蕗屋清一郎が、何故これから記す様な恐ろしい悪事を思立ったか、その動機については詳しいことは分らぬ。又仮令分ったとしてもこのお話には大して関係がないのだ。彼がなかば苦学見たいなことをして、ある大学に通っていた所を見ると、学資の必要に迫られたのかとも考えられる。彼は稀に見る秀才で、而も非常な勉強家だったから、学資を得る為に、つまらぬ内職に時を取られて、好きな読書や思索が十分出来ないのを残念に思っていたのは確かだ。だが、その位の理由で、人間はあんな大罪を犯すものだろうか。恐らく彼は先天的の悪人だったのかも知れない。そして、学資ばかりでなく他の様々な慾望を抑え兼ねたのかも知れない。それは兎も角、彼がそれを思いついてから、もう半年になる。その間、彼は迷いに迷い、考えに考えた揚句、結局やっつけることに決心したのだ。

The Psychological Examination

Through chance events of no importance here, he had previously become friendly with a fellow student named Isamu Saito. This was where things had begun. In the beginning, of course, he had had no ulterior motives. But after a time, he began to draw closer to Saito, nursing a certain hazy goal. And the closer he drew, the more sharply defined that goal became.

For the past year, Saito had been renting a room in a private residence in a lonely residential part of the Yamanote district. The owner of the house was the widow of a government official, but although almost sixty and capable in principle of living quite comfortably by simply renting out the handful of properties her late husband had left her, she found her greatest joy in lending small sums to reliable acquaintances and watching her savings grow from the profits; not having been blessed with children, she said, her money was all she could rely on. She might have rented a room to Saito partly because it was imprudent for a woman to live alone, but there was no doubt that she had included in her calculations the fact that even the rent he paid would increase her savings every month. Indeed, although such things are seldom heard of today, the heart of the miser being unchanging throughout

■ulterior motive 下心　■draw closer 接近していく　■hazy 形おぼろげな
■sum 名金額　■imprudent 形不用心な　■miser 名守銭奴

ある時、彼はふとしたことから、同級生の斎藤勇と親しくなった。それが事の起りだった。初めは無論何の成心があった訳ではなかった。併し中途から、彼はあるおぼろげな目的を抱いて斎藤に接近して行った。そして、接近して行くに随って、そのおぼろげな目的が段々はっきりして来た。

　斎藤は、一年ばかり前から、山の手のある淋しい屋敷町の素人屋に部屋を借りていた。その家の主は、官吏の未亡人で、といっても、もう六十に近い老婆だったが、亡夫の遺して行った数軒の借家から上る利益で、十分生活が出来るにも拘らず、子供を恵まれなかった彼女は、「ただもうお金がたよりだ」といって、確実な知合いに小金を貸したりして、少しずつ貯金を殖して行くのを此上もない楽しみにしていた。斎藤に部屋を貸したのも、一つは女ばかりの暮しでは不用心だからという理由もあっただろうが、一方では部屋代丈けでも、毎月の貯金額が殖えることを勘定に入れていたに相違ない。そして彼女は、今時余り聞かぬ話だけれども、守銭奴の心理は、古今東西を通じて同じものと見える、表面的な銀行預金の外に、莫大な現金を自宅のある秘密な場所へ隠しているという噂だった。

The Psychological Examination

the history of the world, rumor had it that in addition to openly maintaining a savings account she had a large sum of money hidden in a secret location in her home.

This money was a temptation to Fukiya. What merit was there in that old bag possessing such a large sum? Would not the most rational thing be to put it to use paying the school fees of a young man with a future like him? This, in short, was his reasoning. And so, through Saito, he sought to obtain as much information about the old woman as he could. He probed as best he could to discover her secret hiding spot. But he had no firm thoughts on the matter until he heard from Saito that the latter had, by chance, discovered where that hiding spot was.

"Quite ingenious of the old thing, I must admit. Instead of just hiding her money in one of the usual places, like under the verandah or in the attic, she found somewhere a bit more original. Do you know the large potted plant in the display alcove in her drawing room, with the red autumn leaves? The bottom of the pot—that's her hiding place. No burglar would suspect that money might be buried under a potted plant, after all. A genius among misers, eh?"

■old bag ばあさん　■rational 形合理的な　■probe 動〜を徹底的に調べる
■ingenious 形利口な　■attic 名屋根裏　■display alcove 床の間

蕗屋はこの金に誘惑を感じたのだ。あのおいぼれが、そんな大金を持っているということに何の価値がある。それを俺の様な未来のある青年の学資に使用するのは、極めて合理的なことではないか。簡単に云えば、これが彼の理論だった。そこで彼は、斎藤を通じて出来る丈け老婆についての智識を得ようとした。その大金の秘密な隠し場所を探ろうとした。併し彼は、ある時斎藤が、偶然その隠し場所を発見したということを聞くまでは、別に確定的な考を持っていた訳でもなかった。

「君、あの婆さんにしては感心な思いつきだよ、大抵、縁の下とか、天井裏とか、金の隠し場所なんて極っているものだが、婆さんのは一寸意外な所なのだよ。あの奥座敷の床の間に、大きな紅葉の植木鉢が置いてあるだろう。あの植木鉢の底なんだよ。その隠し場所がさ。どんな泥坊だって、まさか植木鉢に金が隠してあろうとは気づくまいからね。婆さんは、まあ云って見れば、守銭奴の天才なんだね」

The Psychological Examination

So said an obviously amused Saito to Fukiya with a laugh.

After this, Fukiya's thoughts gradually became more concrete. He considered all the possibilities at each step along the path that led to the old woman's money being diverted to pay his school fees, striving to come up with the safest possible method. This task was more challenging than he had expected. The most complex mathematical problem was a trifle by comparison. As mentioned earlier, he spent half a year just putting his thoughts in order.

The difficulty, needless to say, lay in evading punishment. He was bothered very little by the ethical impediments to the plan, the prickings of the conscience. Just as he thought it no crime for Napoleon to have murdered on the grand scale that he did—indeed, considered those actions praiseworthy—so too he thought it only natural that a young man of talent should use an old hag who already had one foot in the grave as a sacrificial offering in order to nurture that talent.

The old woman seldom went outside. She spent her days silently huddled in her drawing room. When she did have occasion to leave, her maid from the country

■divert 動 ～を転用する ■striving 動（目的のために）努力する ■trifle 名些細なこと ■evade 動 ～を回避する ■pricking of conscience 良心の咎め ■hag 名鬼婆 ■huddle 動うずくまる

その時、斎藤はこう云って面白そうに笑った。

　それ以来、蕗屋の考は少しずつ具体的になって行った。老婆の金を自分の学資に振替える径路の一つ一つについて、あらゆる可能性を勘定に入れた上、最も安全な方法を考え出そうとした。それは予想以上に困難な仕事だった。これに比べれば、どんな複雑な数学の問題だって、なんでもなかった。彼は先にも云った様に、その考を纏(まと)める丈けの為に半年を費したのだ。

　難点は、云うまでもなく、如何(いか)にして刑罰を免れるかということにあった。倫理上の障礙(しょうがい)、即(すなわ)ち良心の呵責(かしゃく)という様なことは、彼にはさして問題ではなかった。彼はナポレオンの大掛りな殺人を罪悪とは考えないで、寧(むし)ろ讃美すると同じ様に、才能のある青年が、その才能を育てる為に、棺桶に片足をふみ込んだおいぼれを犠牲に供することを、当然だと思った。

　老婆は滅多に外出しなかった。終日黙々として奥の座敷に丸くなっていた。たまに外出することがあっても、留守中は、田舎者の女中が彼女の命を受けて正直に見張番を勤めた。蕗屋のあらゆ

The Psychological Examination

guarded the house diligently upon the old woman's orders. Wrestle with the problem as Fukiya might, the woman's vigilance was flawless. He had initially considered a plan which called for him to fool the maid into leaving her post while the old woman and Saito were out, and then steal the money from the pot in her absence. But this idea was much too risky. If it became known that he had been alone in the house, even for just a moment, would not that alone be sufficient to cast suspicion upon him? He spent a full month contemplating foolish ideas like this, dismissing them almost as soon as they occurred to him. Tricking the old woman into thinking that Saito, the maid, or a regular burglar had stolen the money; sneaking in absolutely silently while the maid was there and stealing the money without being seen; doing the deed at night while the woman was asleep—all these ideas and more he considered. But each and every one contained within it some possibility of discovery.

There was nothing for it but to do the old woman in: such was the awful conclusion at which he finally arrived. How much money the woman actually had was unclear, but considering the matter from several points of view, it seemed unlikely to be a sum great enough to pursue even

★
■diligently 副熱心に　■wrestle with（問題などに）取り組む　■vigilance 名用心　■flawless 形隙がない　■fool ~ into ～を騙して…させる　■contemplate 動熟考する　■deed 名行為

心理試験

　る苦心にも拘らず、老婆の用心には少しの隙もなかった。老婆と斎藤のいない時を見はからって、この女中を騙して使に出すか何かして、その隙に例の金を植木鉢から盗み出したら、蕗屋は最初そんな風に考えて見た。併しそれは甚だ無分別な考だった。仮令少しの間でも、あの家にただ一人でいたことが分っては、もうそれ丈けで十分嫌疑をかけられるではないか。彼はこの種の様々な愚かな方法を、考えては打消し、考えては打消すのに、たっぷり一ヶ月を費した。それは例えば、斎藤か女中か又は普通の泥坊が盗んだと見せかけるトリックだとか、女中一人の時に少しも音を立てないで忍込んで、彼女の目にふれない様に盗み出す方法だとか、夜中、老婆の眠っている間に仕事をする方法だとか、其他考え得るあらゆる場合を、彼は考えた。併し、どれにもこれにも、発覚の可能性が多分に含まれていた。

　どうしても老婆をやっつける外はない。彼は遂にこの恐ろしい結論に達した。老婆の金がどれ程あるかよく分らぬけれど、色々の点から考えて、殺人の危険を犯してまで執着する程大した金額だとは思われぬ。たかの知れた金の為に何の罪もない一人の人間を殺して了うというのは、余りに残酷過ぎはしないか。併し、仮

The Psychological Examination

at the risk of murder. To kill a human being who had committed no crime for a modest sum of money at best: was this not beyond inhuman? And yet, although that sum might not be great by the standards of the world at large, it would be enough to satisfy a poor student like Fukiya. Moreover, according to his thinking, the problem was not the amount of money involved, but rather the task of making discovery of his crime absolutely impossible. In the service of this goal, no sacrifice was too great a price to pay.

At first sight, murder may seem many times more dangerous a deed than mere robbery. But this is a kind of illusion. True, murder committed with the expectation of being discovered would surely be the most dangerous of all crimes. But if one uses difficulty of discovery rather than severity of the crime as the metric, there are cases (for example, those like Fukiya's), in which robbery is the more dangerous deed. On the other hand, killing the discoverer of one's evildoing may be inhuman, but it eliminates concern. Great men have killed and killed without qualm throughout history. Was it not precisely the boldness of their murders that kept them safe from discovery?

❋

■world at large 世間一般の　■at first sight 一見して　■many times more 何倍も　■severity 名重大性　■metric 名測定基準　■qualm 名良心のとがめ

令それが世間の標準から見ては大した金額でなくとも、貧乏な蕗屋には十分満足出来るのだ。のみならず、彼の考によれば、問題は金額の多少ではなくて、ただ犯罪の発覚を絶対に不可能ならしめることだった。その為には、どんな大きな犠牲を払っても、少しも差支ないのだ。

　殺人は、一見、単なる窃盗よりは幾層倍も危険な仕事の様に見える。だが、それは一種の錯覚に過ぎないのだ。成程、発覚することを予想してやる仕事なれば殺人はあらゆる犯罪の中で最も危険に相違ない。併し、若し犯罪の軽重よりも、発覚の難易を目安にして考えたならば、場合によっては（例えば蕗屋の場合の如きは）寧ろ窃盗の方が危い仕事なのだ。これに反して、悪事の発見者をバラして了う方法は、残酷な代りに心配がない。昔から、偉い悪人は、平気でズバリズバリと人殺しをやっている。彼等が却々つかまらぬのは、却ってこの大胆な殺人のお蔭なのではなかろうか。

The Psychological Examination

Very well, then: supposing that the old woman were done away with, would this, indeed, be free of danger? Having arrived at this problem, Fukiya spent several months thinking it through. What ideas did he cultivate over that long period? I will pass over this question here, as the answer will become clear to the reader as our tale progresses, but in any case, through analysis and synthesis that considered every jot and tittle to an extent unthinkable for an ordinary man, he came up with a plan of absolute safety that left not the slightest matter to chance.

Now he had only to wait for his opportunity. This, however, arrived sooner than he had expected, when he became aware one day that both Saito and the maid had left the house, Saito on school business and the maid on an errand, and were certain not to return until evening. This was just two days after Fukiya had finished the last of his preparations. This final act of preparation (this, at least, must be explained in advance) had been a certain act allowing him to confirm that the money's hiding place had not changed in the six months since he had learned it from Saito. On the day he performed this final preparation (which is to say, two days before the old woman's murder), while on a visit to Saito, he had entered

✻

■do away with 排除する　■tale 図物語　■synthesis 図総合　■jot and tittle 微細な点　■errand 図お使い

では、老婆をやっつけるとして、それには果して危険がないか。この問題にぶっつかってから、蕗屋は数ヶ月の間考え通した。その長い間に、彼がどんな風に考を育てて行ったか。それは物語が進むに随って、読者に分ることだから、ここに省くが、兎も角、彼は、到底普通人の考え及ぶことも出来ない程、微に入り細を穿った分析並に綜合の結果、塵一筋の手抜かりもない、絶対に安全な方法を考え出したのだ。

　今はただ、時機の来るのを待つばかりだった。が、それは案外早く来た。ある日、斎藤は学校関係のことで、女中は使に出されて、二人共夕方まで決して帰宅しないことが確められた。それは丁度蕗屋が最後の準備行為を終った日から二日目だった。その最後の準備行為というのは（これ丈けは前以て説明して置く必要がある）嘗つて斎藤に例の隠し場所を聞いてから、もう半年も経過した今日、それがまだ当時のままであるかどうかを確める為の或る行為だった。彼はその日（即ち老婆殺しの二日前）斎藤を訪ねた序に、初めて老婆の部屋である奥座敷に入って、彼女と色々世間話を取交した。彼はその世間話を徐々に一つの方向へ落して行った。そして、屡々老婆の財産のこと、それを彼女がどこかへ隠しているという噂のあることなぞ口にした。彼は「隠す」という言葉の出る毎に、それとなく老婆の眼を注意した。すると、彼女の眼

The Psychological Examination

the old woman's drawing room for the first time and engaged her in conversation on a range of frivolous topics. Gradually he channeled their conversation in a certain direction. He made frequent mention of her savings and the rumor that she had hidden them somewhere, watching her eyes closely each time he said the word "hidden." As expected, each time he did, her gaze darted to the potted plant in the alcove (of course, by then it had been changed from autumn foliage to a miniature pine tree). Repeating this procedure a few times, Fukiya was able to confirm the matter as he had hoped, quickly and leaving no room for the slightest doubt.

は、彼の予期した通り、その都度、床の間の植木鉢（もうその時は紅葉ではなく、松に植えかえてあったけれど）にそっと注がれるのだ。蕗屋はそれを数回繰返して、最早や少しも疑う余地のないことを確めることが出来た。

■frivolous 形取るに足らない　■dart 動サッと動く　■foliage 名木の葉　■no room for 〜の余地がない

The Psychological Examination

II

At last the day arrived. Fukiya donned his school uniform and cap, pulled his student's cape about him, put on an unremarkable pair of gloves, and set off. After much deliberation, he had finally decided against a disguise. To disguise himself would leave a trail of clues that might lead to the discovery of his crime, from his purchase of the materials to the place he had used to change. It would complicate the matter for no real purpose. Crime should be committed in the simplest and plainest manner that was compatible with evading discovery: this was his philosophy, such as it was. All he had to do was ensure that he was not seen entering the house he was about to visit. Even if it became known that he had passed in front of it, this would cause no difficulty. He often took his walk in this area, and could simply say that he had been out for a walk on the day in question as well. On the other hand, if he were seen by an acquaintance en route to his destination (he had no choice but to include

■don 動着用する　■deliberation 名熟考　■decide against 〜しないことに決める　■clue 名手がかり　■compatible 形〜に適している　■en route to 〜へ行く途中で

二

　さて、愈々当日である。彼は大学の正服正帽の上に学生マント を着用し、ありふれた手袋をはめて目的の場所に向った。彼は考 えに考えた上、結局変装しないことに極めたのだ。若し変装をす るとすれば、材料の買入れ、着換えの場所、其他様々の点で、犯 罪発覚の手掛りを残すことになる。それはただ物事を複雑にする ばかりで、少しも効果がないのだ。犯罪の方法は、発覚の虞れの ない範囲に於ては、出来る限り単純に且つあからさまにすべきだ と云うのが、彼の一種の哲学だった。要は、目的の家に入る所を 見られさえしなければいいのだ。仮令その家の前を通ったことが 分っても、それは少しも差支ない。彼はよく其辺を散歩すること があるのだから、当日も散歩をしたばかりだと云い抜けることが 出来る。と同時に一方に於て、彼が目的の家に行く途中で、知合 いの人に見られた場合（これはどうしても勘定に入れて置かねば ならぬ）妙な変装をしている方がいいか、ふだんの通り正服正帽で いる方がいいか、考えて見るまでもないことだ。犯罪の時間につ いても待ちさえすれば都合よい夜が――斎藤も女中も不在の夜が あることは分っているのに、何故彼は危険な昼間を選んだか。こ れも服装の場合と同じく、犯罪から不必要な秘密性を除く為だっ た。

The Psychological Examination

this possibility in his calculations), would he be better off wearing a peculiar disguise, or his usual school uniform? The answer was self-evident. Regarding the timing of the crime, too, why, even knowing that Saito and the maid would be out until late, had he chosen the dangerous daylight hours, rather than simply waiting for the more convenient night to arrive? Just like the matter of his clothing, he sought to eliminate unnecessary secrecy from the crime.

However, as he stood before the house that was his destination, even Fukiya looked around him as anxiously as any regular burglar—no, probably more so. The old woman's house was a freestanding structure separated by hedges from its neighbors on both sides. Beyond it stood a tall concrete wall that ran the length of the street and formed the border of the grounds of a wealthy local family's mansion. The area was a quiet residential one, its streets often empty of passers-by even during the daylight hours. By a stroke of luck, this was the case when Fukiya arrived at the old woman's house; there was not a soul to be seen up and down the street. He let himself in through the grille at the front of the house, opening and closing it with great care to avoid the deafening metallic

■self-evident 形分かりきっている　■freestanding 形独立して建っている　■hedge 名生垣　■passers-by 名通りすがりの人々　■stroke of luck もっけの幸い　■soul 名人　■grille 名格子

併し目的の家の前に立った時だけは、流石の彼も、普通の泥棒の通りに、いや恐らく彼等以上に、ビクビクして前後左右を見廻した。老婆の家は、両隣とは生垣で境した一軒建ちで、向側には、ある富豪の邸宅の高いコンクリート塀が、ずっと一町も続いていた。淋しい屋敷町だから、昼間でも時々はまるで人通りのないことがある。蕗屋がそこへ辿りついた時も、いい塩梅に、通りには犬の子一匹見当らなかった。彼は、普通に開けば馬鹿にひどい金属性の音のする格子戸を、ソロリソロリと少しも音を立てない様に開閉した。そして、玄関の土間から、極く低い声で（これらは隣家への用心だ）案内を乞うた。老婆が出て来ると、彼は、斎藤のことについて少し内密に話し度いことがあるという口実で、奥の間に通った。

The Psychological Examination

shriek it emitted if opened normally. Then, standing in the entryway, he asked extremely quietly (this, too, with the neighbors in mind) if anyone was home. When the old woman appeared, Fukiya talked his way in by telling her that he had come to speak with her privately about Saito.

As soon as Fukiya had sat down, the old woman explained that her maid was absent and turned to make some tea. This was the moment he had been waiting for. As she leaned forward to open the sliding door, he seized her from behind, using the full strength of both hands (he was wearing gloves, but only to avoid leaving finger marks) to strangle her. She offered little resistance, only making a gurgling sound in her throat. As her fingers desperately grasped at the air, however, she brushed against a painted screen and damaged it slightly. It was a two-panel folding screen of considerable vintage, done in gold leaf with vivid color portraits of the Six Saints of Poetry. Her struggling had left an unfortunate tear, just one inch long, on the face of Ono no Komachi.

✤

■shriek 名 鋭い音　■emit 動 発する　■in mind 〜を考慮して　■sliding door 襖　■strangle 動 〜を絞め殺す　■gurgling sound 喉が鳴らす音　■painted screen 屏風

座が定まると間もなく、「あいにく女中が居りませんので」と断りながら、老婆はお茶を汲みに立った。蕗屋はそれを、今か今かと待構えていたのだ。彼は、老婆が襖を開ける為に少し身を屈めた時、やにわに後から抱きついて、両腕を使って（手袋ははめていたけれども、なるべく指の痕はつけまいとしてだ）力まかせに首を絞めた。老婆は咽の所でグッという様な音を出したばかりで、大して藻掻きもしなかった。ただ、苦しまぎれに空を掴んだ指先が、そこに立ててあった屏風に触れて、少しばかり傷を拵えた。それは二枚折の時代のついた金屏風で、極彩色の六歌仙が描かれていたが、その丁度小野の小町の顔の所が、無惨にも一寸許り破れたのだ。

The Psychological Examination

After watching the old woman's breathing cease, Fukiya put the corpse to one side and examined the tear on the screen with a degree of concern. Still, after some thought he concluded that there was nothing to worry about. Something like this could be proof of nothing. He crossed to the alcove, grasped the pine tree at the base of its trunk, and pulled it out of the pot, soil and all. There as expected at the bottom of the pot was a small packet of oiled paper. He calmly opened the packet, produced a large new wallet from his own right pocket, transferred half of the banknotes inside the former (there was at least 5000 yen) into the latter, then returned the wallet to his pocket and put the oiled packet back in the pot with the rest of the money still inside. This, of course, was to conceal the fact that money had been stolen at all. Only the old woman had known how much she had kept here, which meant that even halving the sum should arouse no suspicion.

■corpse 名死体　■oiled paper 油紙《防水性の紙》　■banknote 名紙幣
■conceal 動隠匿する　■arouse 動 〜を喚起する

老婆の息が絶えたのを見定めると、彼は死骸をそこへ横にして、一寸気になる様子で、その屏風の破れを眺めた。併しよく考えて見れば、少しも心配することはない。こんなものが何の証拠になる筈もないのだ。そこで、彼は目的の床の間へ行って、例の松の木の根元を持って、土もろともスッポリと植木鉢から引抜いた。予期した通り、その底には油紙で包んだものが入れてあった。彼は落ちつきはらって、その包みを解いて、右のポケットから一つの新しい大型の財布を取出し、紙幣を半分ばかり（十分五千円はあった）その中に入れると、財布を元のポケットに納め、残った紙幣は油紙に包んで前の通りに植木鉢の底へ隠した。無論、これは金を盗んだという証跡を晦（くら）ます為だ。老婆の貯金の高は、老婆自身が知っていたばかりだから、それが半分になったとて、誰も疑う筈はないのだ。

The Psychological Examination

Next, he balled up a thin sitting cushion and held it to the woman's breast (this was a precaution against blood spattering) before producing a jackknife from his left pocket. He opened the knife and stabbed it into her heart, twisting the blade once before withdrawing it again. Then he used the cushion to wipe the gore off the knife and returned it to his pocket. Strangulation alone, he had reasoned, left open the possibility of recovery. In other words, this was what they used to call the *coup de grace*. Why, then, had he not simply used the blade to begin with? Because he had feared that blood might get on his own clothing.

I must explain at this point about the wallet and jackknife that just made their appearance. He had bought these at an outdoor stall at a festival solely for the use to which they had just been put. Waiting until the busiest time of day at the festival, choosing the busiest stall, and proffering precisely the marked price in exchange for the items, he had slipped away again so quickly that not even the many other festivalgoers, let alone the shopkeeper, had time to remember his face. The items themselves were both entirely unremarkable, lacking any distinguishing features at all.

■ball up（布などを）丸める　■precaution 名予防策　■wipe ~ off ~を拭き取る　■gore 名血のり　■coup de grace とどめの一撃《フランス語》　■stall 名露店　■festivalgoer 名祭りの見物客

それから、彼はそこにあった座蒲団を丸めて老婆の胸にあてがい（これは血潮の飛ばぬ用心だ）左のポケットから一挺のジャックナイフを取出して歯を開くと、心臓をめがけてグサッと突差し、グイと一つ抉（えぐ）って置いて引抜いた。そして、同じ座蒲団の布でナイフの血のりを綺麗に拭き取り、元のポケットへ納めた。彼は、絞め殺しただけでは、蘇生の虞（おそ）れがあると思ったのだ。つまり昔のとどめを刺すという奴だ。では、何故最初から刃物を使用しなかったかというと、そうしてはひょっとして自分の着物に血潮がかかるかも知れないことを虞れたのだ。

　ここで一寸、彼が紙幣を入れた財布と今のジャックナイフについて説明して置かねばならぬ。彼は、それらを、この目的丈けに使う為に、ある縁日の露店で買求めたのだ。彼はその縁日の最も賑う時分を見計らって、最も客の込んでいる店を選び、正札通りの小銭を投出して、品物を取ると、商人は勿論、沢山の客達も、彼の顔を記憶する暇がなかった程、非常に素早く姿を晦（くら）ました。そして、この品物は両方とも、極くありふれた何の目印もあり得ない様なものだった。

The Psychological Examination

 After carefully confirming that he had left nothing behind that could constitute a clue, Fukiya made his way back to the entranceway, not forgetting to close the sliding door behind him. As he was tying his shoelaces, he considered the question of footprints. There was no point in worrying about those any further. The floor of the entranceway was hard stucco, and a streak of fine weather had left the street outside utterly dry. All that remained now was to open the grille and let himself out. But if he should err at this stage, all his pains would have been for nothing. He listened carefully and patiently, trying to discern the sound of footsteps on the street outside. All was quiet and still. The only thing he heard was the supremely tranquil pluck and strum of a *koto* being played indoors somewhere. He mustered his courage and quietly opened the gate. Then, adopting the expression of a caller who has just taken his leave, he stepped nonchalantly into the street. As expected, there was no sign of anyone else.

In that part of the city, every street was of the same quiet residential sort. Four or five streets from the old woman's house was an old stone wall belonging to some shrine or other that ran alongside the road for some

---

■stucco 名漆喰　■streak 名ひと続きの幸運　■err 動しくじる　■tranquil 形静かな　■pluck 動つま弾く　■strum 動かき鳴らす　■nonchalantly 副平然と

さて、蕗屋は、十分注意して少しも手掛りが残っていないのを確めた後、襖のしまりも忘れないでゆっくりと玄関へ出て来た。彼はそこで靴の紐を締めながら、足跡のことを考えて見た。だが、その点は更らに心配がなかった。玄関の土間は堅い漆喰だし、表の通りは天気続きでカラカラに乾いていた。あとには、もう格子戸を開けて表へ出ることが残っているばかりだ。だが、ここでしくじる様なことがあっては、凡ての苦心が水の泡だ。彼はじっと耳を澄して、辛抱強く表通りの跫音を聞こうとした。……しんとして何の気はいもない。どこかの内で琴を弾じる音がコロリンシャンと至極のどかに聞えているばかりだ。彼は思切って、静かに格子戸を開けた。そして、何気なく、今暇をつげたお客様だという様な顔をして、往来へ出た。案の定そこには人影もなかった。

　その一割はどの通りも淋しい屋敷町だった。老婆の家から四五町隔った所に、何かの社の古い石垣が、往来に面してずっと続いていた。蕗屋は、誰も見ていないのを確めた上、そこの石垣の隙間から兇器のジャックナイフと血のついた手袋とを落し込んだ。

The Psychological Examination

distance. Fukiya made sure that no one was watching, then dropped the jackknife that had served as murder weapon and the bloody gloves through a gap in the wall. Then he leisurely strolled to a small park nearby that he had made a habit of frequenting on his walks. He sat on a park bench and spent quite some time watching children play on the swings, his face the picture of tranquility.

On the way home, he stopped at the police station.

"I found this wallet just now," he said, holding out the wallet from earlier. "It seems to have quite a lot in it, so I thought I'd better hand it in."

He answered the questions that followed from the police officer on duty, including the time and place he had found the wallet (his answers here were, of course, plausible but spurious) and his own name and address (here he answered truthfully). Then he received a sort of receipt in the form of a printed card with his name, the sum of money in the wallet, and some other information written on it. There can be no doubt that this was a highly circuitous procedure. However, in terms of safety it was the best. The old woman's money was still in its original location (and no one knew that it had been halved), so there was absolutely no possibility of anyone

★

■leisurely 副のんびりと　■tranquility 名平穏　■hold out ～を差し出す
■plausible 形もっともらしい　■spurious 形嘘の　■circuitous 形遠回りの
■halve 動半分にする

そして、いつも散歩の時には立寄ることにしていた、附近の小さい公園を目ざしてブラブラと歩いて行った。彼は公園のベンチに腰をかけ、子供達がブランコに乗って遊んでいるのを、如何にも長閑(のどか)な顔をして眺めながら、長い時間を過した。

　帰りがけに、彼は警察署へ立寄った。そして、
「今し方、この財布を拾ったのです。大分沢山入っている様ですから、お届けします」

　と云い乍(なが)ら、例の財布をさし出した。彼は巡査の質問に答えて、拾った場所と時間と（勿論それは可能性のある出鱈目なのだ）自分の住所姓名と（これはほんとうの）を答えた。そして、印刷した紙に彼の姓名や金額などを書き入れた受取証見たいなものを貰った。なる程、これは非常に迂遠(うえん)な方法には相違ない。併し安全という点では最上だ。老婆の金は（半分になったことは誰も知らない）ちゃんと元の場所にあるのだから、この財布の遺失主は絶対に出る筈がない。一年の後には間違なく蕗屋の手に落ちるのだ。そして、誰憚らず大びらに使えるのだ。彼は考え抜いた揚句この手段を採った。若しこれをどこかへ隠して置くとするか、どうした偶然から他人に横取りされまいものでもない。自分で持っているか、それはもう考えるまでもなく危険なことだ。のみならず、こ

The Psychological Examination

turning up to claim the wallet. It was certain to fall into his hands a year from now. Then he could spend it openly without fearing what others might think. He had adopted this plan after a great deal of thought. Hiding the money somewhere would have left open the possibility of being relieved of it by another through some coincidence. Holding on to it himself would have been too dangerous even to consider. And this was not all: the plan he had adopted ensured that even on the off chance that the old woman had taken precautions like recording the serial numbers of her banknotes, he himself need not worry in the slightest. (Of course, he had investigated on this point as best he could, and was largely satisfied that no such records existed.)

"Not even Buddha himself would suspect someone who handed something in to the police of having stolen it themselves!" he murmured to himself, holding in his laughter.

The following day, Fukiya woke from his usual restful slumber in his room at the boarding house, opened the newspaper that had been delivered to his bedside, and began to survey the general news pages with a yawn. What he discovered there was unexpected enough to

■fall into someone's hands 〜の手に渡る　■murmur 動呟く　■slumber 图まどろみ

の方法によれば、万一老婆が紙幣の番号を控えていたとしても少しも心配がないのだ。（尤もこの点は出来る丈け探って、大体安心はしていたけれど）

「まさか、自分の盗んだ品物を警察へ届ける奴があろうとは、ほんとうにお釈迦様でも御存じあるまいよ」
　彼は笑いをかみ殺しながら、心の中で呟いた。

　翌日、蕗屋は、下宿の一室で、常と変らぬ安眠から目覚めると、欠伸をしながら、枕許に配達されていた新聞を拡げて、社会面を見渡した。彼はそこに意外な事実を発見して一寸驚いた。だが、それは、決して心配する様な事柄ではなく、却って彼の為には予期しない仕合せだった。というのは、友人の斎藤が嫌疑者として

The Psychological Examination

surprise him somewhat, but not anything that need cause him worry. If anything, it was a stroke of good luck he had not anticipated. For, in fact, Fukiya's friend Saito had been accused of the crime. This accusation, the article reported, was grounded in the fact that Saito had had in his possession a sum of money unsuitably large for one in his position.

"As Saito's closest friend, it would be natural for me to go in to the station and ask them questions about the event."

Fukiya quickly changed his clothes and hurried off to the police station. It was the same station to which he had handed in the wallet the previous day. Why had he not handed the wallet in to a different jurisdiction? This, too, had been intentional, another example of his singular commitment to not overcomplicating matters. With just the right amount of concern in his face, he begged to be allowed to see Saito. As expected, however, his request was refused. At this point he questioned the officer on why Saito should be under suspicion until he had received enough answers to clarify things somewhat.

■accusation 名罪状　■hurry off to 急いで〜へ出かける　■jurisdiction 名管轄(区域)　■overcomplicate 動 〜を必要以上に複雑にする

挙げられたのだ。嫌疑を受けた理由は、彼が身分不相応の大金を所持していたからだと記してある。

「俺は斎藤の最も親しい友達なのだから、ここで警察へ出頭して、色々問い訊(ただ)すのが自然だな」

蕗屋は早速着物を着換えると、遽(あわ)てて警察署へ出掛けた。それは彼が昨日財布を届けたのと同じ役所だ。何故財布を届けるのを管轄の違う警察にしなかったか。いや、それとも亦(また)、彼一流の無技巧(むぎこう)主義で態(わざ)としたことなのだ。彼は、過不足のない程度に心配相な顔をして、斎藤に逢わせて呉れと頼んだ。併し、それは予期した通り許されなかった。そこで、彼は、斎藤が嫌疑を受けた訳を色々と問い訊して、ある程度まで事情を明かにすることが出来た。

The Psychological Examination

This was how he imagined it had happened.

Saito had arrived back at the house yesterday before the maid. This had been just after Fukiya had achieved his objectives and left. As a result, Saito had of course discovered the old woman's body. However, before reporting it to the police, an idea must have come to him: the potted pine. If the murder had been the work of robbers, was the money inside the pot gone? The thought had surely begun as a twinge of curiosity like this. He had checked inside the pot. But to his surprise, the packet of money had still been there. To conceive of wickedness upon seeing this was an imprudent reaction but nevertheless an understandable one. No one knew of that hiding place; it would surely be concluded that the old woman's killer had stolen the money. The strong temptation arising from the circumstances would have been difficult for anyone to resist. What had Saito done next? According to the police, he had come to the police station. But what a foolish man he had been! He had come with the money he had stolen still casually tucked beneath his undercloths. It seemed that he had not imagined that he might be searched on the spot.

■twinge 名 心のうずき　■temptation 名 誘惑　■tuck 動 〜をねじ込む　■on the spot すぐその場で

蕗屋は次の様に想像した。
　昨日、斎藤は女中よりも先に家に帰った。それは蕗屋が目的を果して立去ると間もなくだった。そして、当然老婆の死骸を発見した。併し、直ちに警察に届ける前に、彼はあることを思いついたに相違ない。というのは、例の植木鉢だ。若しこれが盗賊の仕業なれば、或はあの中の金がなくなってはいはしないか。多分それは一寸した好奇心からだったろう。彼はそこを検べて見た。ところが、案外にも金の包(つつみ)がちゃんとあったのだ。それを見て斎藤が悪心を起したのは、実に浅はかな考えではあるが無理もないことだ。その隠し場所は誰れも知らないこと、老婆を殺した犯人が盗んだという解釈が下されるに違いないこと。こうした事情は、誰にしても避け難い強い誘惑に相違ない。それから彼はどうしたか、警官の話では、何食わぬ顔をして人殺しのあったことを警察へ届け出たということだ。ところが、何という無分別な男だ。彼は盗んだ金を腹巻の間へ入れたまま、平気でいたのだ。まさか其場で身体検査をされようとは想像しなかったと見えて。

The Psychological Examination

"But wait. What will Saito say in his defense? Depending on how he proceeds, couldn't things get dangerous?" Fukiya considered this from various angles. When the money had been found on his person, Saito might have claimed that it was his. It was true that no one knew how much had been in the old woman's possession, or where it had been hidden, so this explanation was not obviously impossible. However, was not the sum involved simply too great? Eventually, he would surely admit the truth. But would the court accept it? Barring the emergence of another suspect, Saito was unlikely to escape blame for stealing the money. If all went well for Fukiya, he might be suspected of the murder too. That would settle the matter… but questioning by the judge might bring all sorts of facts to light. For example, the fact that Saito had told Fukiya when he had discovered the money's hiding place, or the fact that Fukiya had had a long conversation with the old woman in her room two days before the crime, or indeed the fact that Fukiya was impoverished and struggling with tuition fees.

★

■barring 前 〜がなければ　■bring 〜 to light 〜を明らかにする
■impoverished 形 貧困にあえぐ

「だが待てよ。斎藤は一体どういう風に弁解するだろう。次第によっては危険なことになりはしないかな」蕗屋はそれを色々と考えて見た。彼は金を見つけられた時、「自分のだ」と答えたかも知れない。なる程老婆の財産の多寡や隠し場所は誰も知らないのだから、一応はその弁明も成立つであろう。併し、金額が余り多すぎるではないか。で、結局彼は事実を申立てることになるだろう。でも、裁判所がそれを承認するかな。外に嫌疑者が出れば兎も角、それまでは彼を無罪にすることは先ずあるまい。うまく行けば、彼が殺人罪に問われるかも知れたものではない。そうなればしめたものだが、……ところで、裁判官が彼を問詰めて行く内に、色々な事実が分って来るだろうな。例えば、彼が金の隠し場所を発見した時に俺に話したことだとか、兇行の二日前に俺が老婆の部屋に入って話込んだことだとか、さては、俺が貧乏で学資にも困っていることだとか。

The Psychological Examination

Fukiya, however, had taken all of this into consideration while making his plans. And rack his brains though he might, he could not imagine any truths more inconvenient for him than these being drawn out of Saito's mouth.

Returning from the police station, Fukiya enjoyed a late breakfast (he spoke of the incident to the maid who brought him his repast) before going to school as usual. Rumors of Saito were the only topic of conversation there. Somewhat smugly, Fukiya took his place at the center of these conversations.

併し、これらは皆、蕗屋がこの計画を立てる前に予め勘定に入れて置いたことばかりだった。そして、どんなに考えても、斎藤の口からそれ以上彼にとって不利な事実が引出されようとは考えられなかった。

蕗屋は警察から帰ると、遅れた朝食を認（したた）めて（その時食事を運んで来た女中に事件について話して聞かせたりした）いつもの通り学校へ出た。学校では斎藤の噂で持切りだった。彼はなかば得意気にその噂話の中心になって喋った。

■rack one's brains 頭を働かせる　■repast 名 食事　■smugly 副 得意気に

心理試験

III

Now, esteemed readers, I am sure that those of you familiar with the nature of the detective novel know full well that the story does not end here. Nor does it indeed. In fact, everything up to this point has been a mere prelude to the story, and it is what comes next that I most wish you to read: the sequence of events in which Fukiya's carefully planned crimes were uncovered.

The magistrate assigned to this case was the renowned Judge Kasamori. Not only was he known as a fine judge in the usual sense, he was even more famous for a certain unusual predilection. The judge was an amateur psychologist of a sort, and when faced with cases that resisted the usual methods of judgment had many times arrived at a solution by employing his wealth of psychological knowledge instead. His experience was yet shallow, his years were few, but his genius was so great that his position as a regional court magistrate almost seemed a waste. The case of the murdered old woman

■esteemed 形尊敬すべき　■nature 名性質　■magistrate 名判事
■predilection 名特別の好み　■shallow 形浅い

三

　さて読者諸君、探偵小説というものの性質に通暁せらるる諸君は、お話は決してこれ切りで終らぬことを百も御承知であろう。如何にもその通りである。実を云えばここまでは、この物語の前提に過ぎないので、作者が是非、諸君に読んで貰い度いと思うのは、これから後なのである。つまり、かくも企らんだ蕗屋の犯罪が如何にして発覚したかというそのいきさつについてである。

　この事件を担当した予審判事は、有名な笠森氏であった。彼は普通の意味で名判事だったばかりでなく、ある多少風変りな趣味を持っているので一層有名だった。それは、彼が一種の素人心理学者だったことで、彼は普通のやり方ではどうにも判断の下し様がない事件に対しては、最後に、その豊富な心理学上の智識を利用して、屢々奏効した。彼は経歴こそ浅く、年こそ若かったけれど、地方裁判所の一予審判事としては、勿体ない程の俊才だった。今度の老婆殺し事件も、笠森判事の手にかかれば、もう訳なく解決することと、誰しも考えていた。当の笠森氏自身も同じ様に考えた。いつもの様に、この事件も、予審廷ですっかり調べ上げて、公判の場合にはいささかの面倒も残っていぬ様に処理してやろう

The Psychological Examination

now having fallen into Judge Kasamori's hands, everyone expected that it would be resolved without incident. The judge himself assumed the same. He intended to pursue his usual strategy of investigating the incident so thoroughly in the preliminary hearings that the trial itself would proceed without a hint of inconvenience.

However, as his investigations proceeded, he gradually became aware of difficulties with the case. The police's position was simple: Isamu Saito was guilty. Judge Kasamori did not deny that this made a certain amount of sense. After all, even after summoning everyone known to have visited the woman's house while she was alive and investigating them thoroughly, be they debtors, renters, or simply acquaintances, not a single suspicious individual had been found. Seiichiro Fukiya was, of course, among their number. If no other suspect emerged, there would be no option but to assume for the time being that Isamu Saito, the most suspicious of the lot, was the murderer. And this was not all. The most inconvenient thing for Saito was that he was timid by nature, so petrified by the court atmosphere that he was unable to respond clearly and crisply to questioning. Flustered, he took back earlier statements, forgot things he ought to have known, and blurted out inconvenient facts for no good reason—and

★

■preliminary hearing 予審　■debtor 图債務者　■petrify 動すくみ上がらせる
■crisply 副歯切れよく　■blurt out 思わず〜を言う

と思っていた。

　ところが、取調を進めるに随って、事件の困難なことが段々分って来た。警察署等は単純に斎藤勇の有罪を主張した。笠森判事とても、その主張に一理あることを認めないではなかった。というのは生前老婆の家に出入りした形跡のある者は、彼女の債務者であろうが、借家人であろうが、単なる知合であろうが、残らず召喚して綿密に取調べたにも拘らず、一人として疑わしい者はないのだ。蕗屋清一郎も勿論その内の一人だった。外に嫌疑者が現れぬ以上、さしずめ最も疑うべき斎藤勇を犯人と判断する外はない。のみならず、斎藤にとって最も不利だったのは、彼が生来気の弱い質で、一も二もなく法廷の空気に恐れをなして了って、訊問に対してもハキハキ答弁の出来なかったことだ。のぼせ上った彼は、屡々以前の陳述を取消したり、当然知っている筈の事を忘れて了ったり、云わずともの不利な申立をしたり、あせればあせる程、益々嫌疑を深くする計だった。それというのも、彼には老婆の金を盗んだという弱味があったからで、それさえなければ、相当頭のいい斎藤のことだから如何に気が弱いといって、あの様なへまな真似はしなかっただろうに、彼の立場は実際同情すべきものだった。併し、それでは斎藤を殺人犯と認めるかという

The Psychological Examination

the more desperate he grew, the more strongly he was suspected. Even this was because of his chief weakness, which was having stolen the old woman's money; if not for this, timid as Saito was, his intelligence should have helped him avoid acting this way. He was in a truly pitiable position. However, as to whether Saito was the killer, Judge Kasamori could not be so confident. Here there was only suspicion. There had been no confession from Saito, of course, or any other proof to speak of.

In this way one month passed. The preliminary hearings were still ongoing. The judge began to feel the pressure. It was at this juncture that the chief of police in the jurisdiction where the old woman had been murdered made an intriguing report to him. It seemed that on the day of the incident, a wallet containing just over five thousand yen had been found on a street not far from the old woman's house by one Seiichiro Fukiya, fellow student and close friend of the suspect Saito, but that this fact had hitherto gone overlooked due to the carelessness of the person in charge of the case. However, the chief concluded, there had to be some explanation for such a large sum of money going unclaimed for an entire month, and so he had reported the matter just in case.

■chief 形 根本的な　■juncture 名 時点　■intriguing 形 興味をそそる
■hitherto 副 今まで　■in charge of ～を担当して　■just in case 念の為に

と、笠森氏にはどうもその自信がなかった。そこにはただ疑いがあるばかりなのだ。本人は勿論自白せず、外にこれという確証もなかった。

　こうして、事件から一ヶ月が経過した。予審はまだ終結しない。判事は少しあせり出していた。丁度その時、老婆殺しの管轄の警察署長から、彼の所へ一つの耳よりな報告が齎らされた。それは事件の当日五千二百何十円在中の一個の財布が、老婆の家から程遠からぬ──町に於て拾得されたが、その届主が、嫌疑者の斎藤の親友である蕗屋清一郎という学生だったことを、係りの者の疎漏から今日まで気附かずにいた。が、その大金の遺失者が一ヶ月たっても現れぬ所を見ると、そこに何か意味がありはしないか。念の為に御報告するということだった。

The Psychological Examination

The stumped Judge Kasamori received the report like a ray of light. The process of summoning Seiichiro Fukiya was begun at once. However, despite the judge's enthusiasm, questioning Fukiya was of little benefit. Asked why he had not mentioned finding the money during his initial questioning regarding the incident, he answered that he had not thought it connected to the murder. The reasoning behind this excuse was sound. The old woman's life savings had been found in Saito's underclothes—who would suppose any other money, much less money found on the street, to be part of those savings as well?

Was this, however, a coincidence? Was it truly a coincidence that, on the day of the incident, not far from the scene of the crime, a close friend of the prime suspect (who, according to Saito's statement, knew of the hiding place in the potted pine) should find such a large sum of money in the street? The judge racked his brains trying to uncover some meaning in the facts. It was most regrettable, he thought, that the old woman had not recorded the serial numbers of her banknotes. If such a record had been available, it could be determined at once whether this suspicious money was connected to the incident or not.

★

■stump 動途方に暮れさせる ■sound 形理にかなった ■scene of a crime 犯行現場 ■prime suspect 有力な容疑者 ■regrettable 形悔やまれる

困り抜いていた笠森判事は、この報告を受取って、一道の光明を認めた様に思った。早速蕗屋清一郎召喚の手続が取り運ばれた。ところが、蕗屋を訊問した結果は、判事の意気込みにも拘らず、大して得る所もない様に見えた。何故、事件の当時取調べた際、その大金拾得の事実を申立てなかったかという訊問に対して、彼は、それが殺人事件に関係があるとは思わなかったからだと答えた。この答弁には十分理由があった。老婆の財産は斎藤の腹巻の中から発見されたのだから、それ以外の金が、殊に往来に遺失されていた金が、老婆の財産の一部だと誰れが想像しよう。

　併し、これが偶然であろうか。事件の当日、現場から余り遠くない所で、しかも第一の嫌疑者の親友である男が（斎藤の申立によれば彼は植木鉢の隠し場所をも知っていたのだ）この大金を拾得したというのが、これが果して偶然であろうか。判事はそこに何かの意味を発見しようとして悶えた。判事の最も残念に思ったのは、老婆が紙幣の番号を控えて置かなかったことだ。それさえあれば、この疑わしい金が、事件に関係があるかないかも、直ちに判明するのだが。

The Psychological Examination

"If I could just find one solid clue, no matter how small," the judge mused, straining his genius to the limit. The scene of the crime had been examined repeatedly. The old woman's familial relations had been probed in full. Nothing had been found. In this way another fruitless half-month passed.

There was just one possibility, the judge thought. Suppose that Fukiya had stolen half of the old woman's savings, returned the rest to their original hiding place, put the stolen money in the wallet, and then pretended to have found the wallet on the street. Did such foolishness make sense, however? The wallet had of course been examined, but no clues to speak of had been found. And had not Fukiya himself openly acknowledged passing the old woman's house on his walk the day of the incident, in his statements? Would the guilty party act so boldly? In any case, the whereabouts of the murder weapon, the most important data point, was unknown. A search of Fukiya's lodgings had borne no fruit whatsoever. But did not this lack of a murder weapon apply equally to Saito's case? Who, then, was to be suspected?

There was no hard proof to speak of. If one followed the lead of the chief of police and suspected Saito, Saito

---

■muse 動 熟考する   ■strain 動 〜を研ぎ澄ます   ■make sense 道理にかなう
■guilty party 犯人   ■bear no fruit 何の結果ももたらさない

「どんな小さなことでも、何か一つ確かな手掛りを掴みさえすればなあ」判事は全才能を傾けて考えた。現場の取調べも幾度となく繰返された。老婆の親族関係も十分調査した。併し何の得る所もない。そうして又半月ばかり徒(いたず)らに経過した。

たった一つの可能性は、と判事が考えた。蕗屋が老婆の貯金を半分盗んで、残りを元通りに隠して置き、盗んだ金を財布に入れて、往来で拾った様に見せかけたと推定することだ。だが、そんな馬鹿なことがあり得るだろうか。その財布も無論検べて見たけれど、これという手掛りもない。それに、蕗屋は平気で、当日散歩のみちすがら、老婆の家の前を通ったと申立てているではないか。犯人にこんな大胆なことが云えるものだろうか。第一、最も大切な兇器の行方が分らぬ。蕗屋の下宿の家宅捜索の結果は、何物をも齎(もた)らさなかったのだ。併し、兇器のことをいえば、斎藤とても同じではないか。では一体誰れを疑ったらいいのだ。

そこには確証というものが一つもなかった。署長等の云う様に、斎藤を疑えば斎藤らしくもある。だが又、蕗屋とても疑って疑え

did appear suspicious. But if one shifted one's suspicion to Fukiya, that looked plausible too. What the judge did know was that a month and a half spent investigating every angle possible had turned up no suspects whatsoever other than these two. Every avenue had been exhausted. It was time, he decided, to bring out his reserves. He resolved to perform one of his psychological examinations, which had proven so successful in previous cases, on the two suspects.

IV

When Fukiya received his first summons two or three days after the incident, he learned that the presiding magistrate would be the renowned amateur psychologist Judge Kasamori. Foreseeing even then the possibility that things would end as indeed they did, he suffered no small consternation. Even Fukiya had not imagined that psychological examinations might be held in Japan, even as individual diversions. From reading widely, he already knew all too well what a psychological cxamination involved.

■bring out one's reserve 奥の手を出す　■presiding 議長を務める
■consternation 狼狽

ぬことはない。ただ、分っているのは、この一ヶ月半のあらゆる捜索の結果、彼等二人を除いては、一人の嫌疑者も存在しないということだった。万策尽きた笠森判事は愈々奥の手を出す時だと思った。彼は二人の嫌疑者に対して、彼の従来屡々成功した心理試験を施そうと決心した。

四

蕗屋清一郎は、事件の二三日後に第一回目の召喚を受けた際、係りの予審判事が有名な素人心理学者の笠森氏だということを知った。そして、当時已(すで)にこの最後の場合を予想して少なからず狼狽(ろうばい)した。流石の彼も、日本に仮令一個人の道楽気からとは云え、心理試験などというものが行われていようとは想像していなかった。彼は、種々の書物によって、心理試験の何物であるかを、知り過ぎる程知っていたのだ。

The Psychological Examination

Having at this great blow already lost the poise which had allowed him to continue attending school as before, he pleaded illness and shut himself inside his rented quarters. There he devoted himself solely to the problem of how he might pass through this narrow gate. His thinking was as scrupulous and fervent as it had been before committing the murder, if not more so.

What kind of psychological examination would Judge Kasamori perform? There was absolutely no way to know. So Fukiya recalled all of the methods he knew of, and considered how he might handle each one in turn. However, the very point of a psychological examination being to detect false statements, deceiving the examination itself seemed a logical impossibility.

As Fukiya saw it, psychological examinations could be broadly divided into two types according to their nature. The first type relied purely on biological responses, while the second was conducted verbally. In the former case, the examiner sought to uncover truths that normal interrogation could not uncover by posing a variety of questions relating to the crime and using some appropriate apparatus to record the minute bodily reactions of the subject. The theory behind this was that a human

★
■poise 名冷静　■scrupulous 形綿密な　■fervent 形熱心な　■verbally 副言葉によって　■interrogation 名尋問　■appropriate 形ふさわしい　■apparatus 名装置

この大打撃に、最早や平気を装って通学を続ける余裕を失った彼は、病気と称して下宿の一室にとじ籠った。そして、ただ、如何にしてこの難関を切抜けるべきかを考えた。丁度、殺人を実行する以前にやったと同じ、或はそれ以上の、綿密と熱心を以て考え続けた。

　笠森判事は果してどの様な心理試験を行うであろうか。それは到底予知することが出来ない。で、蕗屋は知っている限りの方法を思出して、その一つ一つについて、何とか対策がないものかと考えて見た。併し、元来心理試験というものが、虚偽の申立をあばく為に出来ているのだから、それを更らに偽るということは、理論上不可能らしくもあった。

　蕗屋の考によれば、心理試験はその性質によって二つに大別することが出来た。一つは純然たる生理上の反応によるもの、今一つは言葉を通じて行われるものだ。前者は、試験者が犯罪に関聯した様々の質問を発して、被験者の身体上の微細な反応を、適当な装置によって記録し、普通の訊問によっては、到底知ることの出来ない真実を掴もうとする方法だ。それは、人間は、仮令言葉の上で、又は顔面表情の上で嘘をついても、神経そのものの興奮は隠すことが出来ず、それが微細な肉体上の徴候として現われるものだという理論に基くので、その方法としては、例(たと)えば、

The Psychological Examination

being might lie in words or even with their expression, but they could not hide the excitement of their nervous system itself, which would manifest itself as many forms of subtle bodily response. For example, one might use an automatograph to discover subtle movements of the hand. One might employ certain methods to measure the movement of the eyeballs. One might measure the depth and speed of breathing with a pneumograph. One might measure blood pressure and pulse with a sphygmograph. One might measure blood levels in the limbs with a plethysmograph. One might measure subtle perspiration on the palm with a galvanometer. One might check how much the muscles contracted after a light tap on the knee. All these methods and others were conceivable.

If, for example, he was suddenly accused of having killed the old woman himself, he was confident that he would be able to maintain a calm expression as he asked "On what basis do you make that accusation?" At that moment, however, might not his pulse rise unnaturally, or his breath quicken? Was preventing such things not an absolute impossibility? He ran experiments in his mind based on various imagined scenarios. Mysteriously, however, no matter how suddenly he posed questions

★
■automatograph 图自動運動記録装置 ■pneumograph 图呼吸運動記録装置
■sphygmograph 图脈波計 ■plethysmograph 图容積脈波記録装置
■perspiration 图発汗 ■galvanometer 图検流計

Automatographなどの力を借りて、手の微細な動きを発見する方法。ある手段によって眼球の動き方を確める方法。Pneumographによって呼吸の深浅遅速を計る方法。Sphygmographによって脈搏の高低遅速を計る方法。Plethysmographによって四肢の血量を計る方法。Galvanometerによって掌の微細なる発汗を発見する方法。膝の関節を軽く打って生ずる筋肉の収縮の多少を見る方法、其他これらに類した種々様々の方法がある。

例えば、不意に「お前は老婆を殺した本人であろう」と問われた場合、彼は平気な顔で「何を証拠にそんなことをおっしゃるのです」と云い返す丈けの自信はある。だが、その時不自然に脈搏が高まったり、呼吸が早くなる様なことはないだろうか。それを防ぐことは絶対に不可能なのではあるまいか。彼は色々な場合を仮定して、心の内で実験して見た。ところが、不思議なことには、自分自身で発した訊問は、それがどんなにきわどい、不意の思付きであっても、肉体上に変化を及ぼす様には考えられなかった。無論微細な変化を計る道具がある訳ではないから、確かなことは云

The Psychological Examination

to himself, and no matter how closely those questions approached the truth, he could not sense any bodily responses. He did not have any equipment that could measure microscopic changes, of course, and so could not speak with certainty, but if he did not feel any excitation in his nerves, bodily changes resulting from such should not arise either.

As he continued his various experiments and projections, Fukiya arrived abruptly at a certain thought: might not practice itself thwart the effectiveness of a psychological examination? That is to say, might not the nerves react more weakly to a question the second time they heard it, and more weakly still the third? One might, in other words, accustom oneself to the examination. As reflection upon a range of other cases should make clear, the possibility of this is high. Surely this was the ultimate cause behind his lack of reaction to questions he asked himself: he knew what the questions would be before they were asked.

And so he read through every single one of the tens of thousands of words in the *Jirin* dictionary, copying out all those that had a chance of appearing in the questions he might be asked, no matter how slight that chance was.

■projection 名予測　■thwart 動〜を阻害する　■accustom 動慣れさせる
■copy out 完全に書き写す

えぬけれど、神経の興奮そのものが感じられない以上は、その結果である肉体上の変化も起らぬ筈だった。

　そうして、色々と実験や推量を続けている内に、蕗屋はふとある考にぶっつかった。それは、練習というものが心理試験の効果を妨げはしないか、云い換えれば、同じ質問に対しても、一回目よりは二回目が、二回目よりは三回目が、神経の反応が微弱になりはしないかということだった。つまり、慣れるということだ。これは他の色々の場合を考えて見ても分る通り、随分可能性がある。自分自身の訊問に対して反応がないというのも、結局はこれと同じ理窟で、訊問が発せられる以前に、已に予期がある為に相違ない。

　そこで、彼は「辞林」の中の何万という単語を一つも残らず調べて見て、少しでも訊問され相な言葉をすっかり書き抜いた。そして、一週間もかかって、それに対する神経の「練習」をやった。

The Psychological Examination

He then spent a full week "training" his nerves against that list.

Next was the method of examination through words. There was nothing to fear here. On the contrary, the medium being words just made deception easier. There were various methods, but the most common was the one known as "free association," which was used by analysts on their patients. Words with no particular import, such as "glass" or "desk" or "ink" or "pen," were read aloud one after the other, with the patient responding to each by speaking aloud the first word that came into their own head as a result. For example, in response to "glass" any number of words might occur to the subject, from "window" or "sill" to "paper" or "door." It did not matter what the subject's reply was as long as it was the first one that came to mind. Into this procedure the examiner would surreptitiously mix words related to the crime, like "knife" or "blood" or "money" or "wallet," in order to probe the associations that arose therefrom.

First of all, the most shallow thinkers among the subjects of such an examination might, in response to the word "pot" in the context of the old woman's murder, unthinkingly respond "money." In other words, stealing

■medium 名媒体となるもの　■deception 名ごまかし　■sill 名敷居
■surreptitiously 副気づかれないように　■context 名前後関係

さて次には、言葉を通じて試験する方法だ。これとても恐れることはない。いや寧ろ、それが言葉である丈けごまかし易いというものだ。これには色々な方法があるけれど、最もよく行われるのは、あの精神分析家が病人を見る時に用いるのと同じ方法で、聯想診断という奴だ。「障子」だとか「机」だとか「インキ」だとか「ペン」だとか、なんでもない単語をいくつも順次に読み聞かせて、出来る丈け早く、少しも考えないで、それらの単語について聯想した言葉を喋らせるのだ。例えば、「障子」に対しては「窓」とか「敷居」とか「紙」とか「戸」とか色々の聯想があるだろうが、どれでも構わない、その時ふと浮んだ言葉を云わせる。そして、それらの意味のない単語の間へ、「ナイフ」だとか「血」だとか「金」だとか「財布」だとか、犯罪に関係のある単語を、気づかれぬ様に混ぜて置いて、それに対する聯想を検べるのだ。

　先ず第一に、最も思慮の浅い者は、この老婆殺しの事件で云えば「植木鉢」という単語に対して、うっかり「金」と答えるかも知れない。即ち「植木鉢」の底から「金」を盗んだことが最も深く印象されているからだ。そこで彼は罪状を自白したことになる。だ

The Psychological Examination

the *money* from the bottom of the *pot* had made the deepest impression upon them. At that point, such a subject would have confessed his own guilt. However, someone who thought slightly more deeply would probably, even if the word "money" came to him in response to "pot," push it back down and respond with "Seto porcelain" or the like.

There were two methods for preventing dissimulation of this sort. The first was to repeat a word that had previously been tested after allowing a short amount of time to pass. A spontaneous response would usually be identical both times, but a crafted response would, nine times out of ten, differ the second time. For example, in response to "pot," the first answer might be "Seto porcelain" and the second "earth."

The other method was to use special equipment to precisely record the time between asking questions and obtaining answers, and then examine the differences in response times. For example, if the response "door" had come one second after giving the word "screen," but "Seto porcelain" had taken three seconds in response to the word "pot" (in reality, the times would not be

■push ~ back down （言葉などを）押し殺す　■porcelain 図磁器
■dissimulation 図偽ること　■spontaneous 形自然発生的な　■earth 図土
■nine times out of ten 十中八九

が、少し考え深い者だったら、仮令「金」という言葉が浮んでも、それを押し殺して、例えば「瀬戸物」と答えるだろう。

　斯様(かよう)な偽(いつわ)りに対して二つの方法がある。一つは、一巡試験した単語を、少し時間を置いて、もう一度繰返すのだ。すると、自然に出た答は多くの場合前後相違がないのに、故意に作った答は、十中八九は最初の時と違って来る。例えば「植木鉢」に対しては最初は「瀬戸物」と答え、二度目は「土」と答える様なものだ。

　もう一つの方法は、問を発してから答を得るまでの時間を、ある装置によって精確に記録し、その遅速によって、例えば「障子」に対して「戸」と答えた時間が一秒間であったにも拘らず、「植木鉢」に対して「瀬戸物」と答えた時間が三秒間もかかったとすれば（実際はこんな単純なものではないけれど）それは「植木鉢」について最初に現れた聯想を押し殺す為に時間を取ったので、その被験者は怪しいということになるのだ。この時間の遅延は、当面の単語

The Psychological Examination

so simple), that might mean that the subject had taken some time to push down the first association that had appeared in response to "pot," a suspicious thing to do. Such variation in response time might also be observed for the meaningless words immediately following the true key words, rather than the key words themselves.

The other method involved telling the subject the circumstances of the crime in detail and then having them repeat what they had heard. If they were the true culprit, their version of events would differ in certain fine details from what they had been told, because they would unthinkingly speak the truth rather than repeating what they had heard. (I must apologize to readers with some knowledge of psychological examinations for this belabored account. However, if I were to leave these details out, the story as a whole would become quite unclear to other readers, and so I have no choice but to include them.)

It went without saying that practice was just as necessary for examinations of this type as it was for the types mentioned earlier. However, what was even more important in Fukiya's opinion was guilelessness. One could not rely on tiresome tricks.

★

■unthinkingly 副うっかりと　■belabor 動長々と論じる　■leave ~ out ～を省略する　■guilelessness 名無邪気さ

に現れないで、その次の意味のない単語に現れることもある。

　又、犯罪当時の状況を詳しく話して聞かせて、それを復誦(ふくしょう)させる方法もある。真実の犯人であったら、復誦する場合に、微細な点で、思わず話して聞かされたことと違った真実を口走って了うものなのだ。（心理試験について知っている読者に、余りにも煩瑣(はんさ)な叙述をお詫(わ)びせねばならぬ。が、若しこれを略する時は、外の読者には、物語全体が曖昧になって了うのだから、実に止むを得なかったのである）

　この種の試験に対しては、前の場合と同じく「練習」が必要なのは云うまでもないが、それよりももっと大切なのは、蕗屋に云わせると、無邪気なことだ。つまらない技巧を弄(ろう)しないことだ。

The Psychological Examination

In response to the word "pot," to immediately say "money" or "pine" would in fact be the safest procedure. After all, even if Fukiya had not been the perpetrator, it would only be natural for him to have acquired a certain familiarity with the facts of the crime through the investigations of the judge and other routes. This being so, would not the fact of the money at the bottom of the pot have made the most recent and deepest impression on him, making it entirely natural for his free associations to be influenced in that manner? (Avoiding unnecessary dissimulation was also the safest policy when one was made to repeat the details of the crime scene.) Response time was the only problem. Here, too, practice would be necessary. He would have to practice until he could reply "money" or "pine" when "pot" came up without becoming flustered even in the slightest. He spent several additional days on this practice. With this, his preparations were complete.

His calculations also took account of one respect in which matters were in his favor, to the extent that even if he were faced with questions he had not anticipated, or, worse yet, exhibited a disadvantageous response to

■tiresome 形つまらない　■perpetrator 名犯人　■fluster 動まごつく　■take account of 〜を考慮に入れる

「植木鉢」に対しては、寧ろあからさまに「金」又は「松」と答えるのが、一番安全な方法なのだ。というのは蕗屋は仮令彼が犯人でなかったとしても、判事の取調べその他によって、犯罪事実をある程度まで知悉しているのが当然だから。そして、植木鉢の底に金があったという事実は、最近の且つ最も深刻な印象に相違ないのだから、聯想作用がそんな風に働くのは至極あたり前ではないか。（又、この手段によれば、現場の有様を復誦させられた場合にも安全なのだ）唯、問題は時間の点だ。これには矢張り「練習」が必要である。「植木鉢」と来たら、少しもまごつかないで、「金」又は「松」と答え得る様に練習して置く必要がある。彼は更らにこの「練習」の為に数日を費した。斯様にして、準備は全く整った。

　彼は又、一方に於て、ある一つの有利な事情を勘定に入れていた。それを考えると、仮令、予期しない訊問に接しても、更らに一歩を進めて、予期した訊問に対して不利な反応を示しても毫も恐れることはないのだった。というのは、試験されるのは、蕗屋

The Psychological Examination

a question he had, he would still have nothing to fear. That advantage was this: the psychological examination would not be performed on Fukiya alone. Innocent of the deed itself as he might be, could the psychologically oversensitive Isamu Saito maintain unruffled equanimity in the face of a battery of questions? Would it not be more natural for him to exhibit reactions on at least the same level as Fukiya?

The more Fukiya considered the matter, the more confident he felt. He almost felt like humming. Not only did he no longer dread the prospect of a summons from Judge Kasamori, he eagerly anticipated it.

V

How did Judge Kasamori conduct his psychological examination? What responses did the nervous Saito exhibit? To what extent did Fukiya maintain his composure during the testing? Rather than offering a tiresome blow-by-blow account of the events, I shall proceed at once to discussion of what resulted from them.

■unruffled 形落ち着いた　■equanimity 名平静　■more ~, the more ~すればするほどますます…　■blow-by-blow 形事細かな

一人ではないからだ。あの神経過敏な斎藤勇がいくら身に覚えがないといって、様々の訊問に対して、果して虚心平気でいることが出来るだろうか。恐らく、彼とても、少くとも蕗屋と同様位の反応を示すのが自然ではあるまいか。

蕗屋は考えるに随って、段々安心して来た。何だか鼻唄でも歌い出したい様な気持になって来た。彼は今は却って、笠森判事の呼出しを待構える様にさえなった。

五

笠森判事の心理試験が如何様に行われたか。それに対して、神経家の斎藤がどんな反応を示したか。蕗屋が、如何に落ちつきはらって試験に応じたか。ここにそれらの管々（くだくだ）しい叙述を並べ立てることを避けて、直ちにその結果に話を進めることにする。

The Psychological Examination

It was the morning after the psychological examinations had been completed. Judge Kasamori was in his study, head bowed in contemplation of the experimental results recorded on the papers spread out before him, when the calling card of one Kogoro Akechi was brought in.

Those who have read "The Case of the Murder on D Hill" will know something of what sort of man this Kogoro Akechi was. After the events of that story, he exercised his rare genius in connection with many criminal cases, and met with warm acclaim from not only experts but also the world at large. As luck would have it, he had also become friendly with Judge Kasamori following a certain incident not long ago.

The maid led the smiling Akechi into the judge's study. This story takes place several years after "The Case of the Murder on D Hill," and Akechi was no longer the student of those days.

"Assiduous as always, I see."

Akechi peered at the papers on the judge's desk as he spoke.

■contemplation 図黙考　■calling card 名刺　■acclaim 図称賛　■assiduous 形根気強い

それは心理試験が行われた翌日のことである。笠森判事が、自宅の書斎で、試験の結果を書きとめた書類を前にして、小首を傾けている所へ、明智小五郎の名刺が通じられた。

　「D坂の殺人事件」を読んだ人は、この明智小五郎がどんな男だかということを、幾分御存じであろう。彼はその後、屢々困難な犯罪事件に関係して、その珍らしい才能を現し、専門家達は勿論一般の世間からも、もう立派に認められていた。笠森氏ともある事件から心易くなったのだ。

　女中の案内につれて、判事の書斎に、明智のニコニコした顔が現れた。このお話は「D坂の殺人事件」から数年後のことで、彼ももう昔の書生ではなくなっていた。

　「却々、御精が出ますね」
　明智は判事の机の上を覗きながら云った。

The Psychological Examination

"I must admit that this one has me quite flummoxed." The judge turned to face his visitor as he replied.

"The murder of that old woman, I presume? How were the results of the psychological examination?"

Akechi had learned the details of the case from Judge Kasamori over the course of several meetings since the incident.

"Oh, the results are quite clear," the judge said. "And yet for some reason I find them difficult to accept. I performed a pulse test and free association examination yesterday. Fukiya showed barely any response. There were some rather suspicious moments during the pulse test, but even those were too minor to notice compared to Saito's responses. Look at this. It's a record of questions and pulse rates. As you can see, Saito's responses are quite extreme. The same was true of the free association test. It's obvious just from looking at the response time for the stimulus word 'pot.' Fukiya's response to that word comes even faster than his response to the meaningless ones, but look at Saito—he takes six whole seconds!"

The judge showed Akechi the results of the free association test, included below.

■flummox 動 ～を困惑させる　■presume 動 ～と思う　■pulse 名 脈拍
■stimulus word 刺激語

「イヤ、どうも、今度はまったく弱りましたよ」
　判事が、来客の方に身体の向きを換えながら応じた。
「例の老婆殺しの事件ですね。どうでした、心理試験の結果は」

　明智は、事件以来、度々笠森判事に逢って詳しい事情を聞いていたのだ。

「イヤ、結果は明白ですがね」と判事「それがどうも、僕には何だか得心出来ないのですよ。昨日は脈搏の試験と聯想診断をやって見たのですが、蕗屋の方は殆ど反応がないのです。尤も脈搏では、大分疑わしい所もありましたが、併し、斎藤に比べれば、問題にもならぬ位僅かなんです。これを御覧なさい。ここに質問事項と、脈搏の記録がありますよ。斎藤の方は実に著しい反応を示しているでしょう。聯想試験でも同じことです。この『植木鉢』という刺戟語に対する反応時間を見ても分りますよ。蕗屋の方は外の無意味な言葉よりも却って短い時間で答えているのに斎藤の方は、どうです、六秒もかかっているじゃありませんか」

　判事が示した聯想診断の記録は左の様に記されていた。

The Psychological Examination

	Stimulus word	Seiichiro Fukiya		Isamu Saito	
		Response word	Response time	Response word	Response time
	Head	Hair	0.9 s	Tail	1.2 s
	Green	Blue	0.7	Blue	1.1
	Water	Bath	0.9	Fish	1.3
	Sing	Song	1.1	Woman	1.5
	Long	Short	1.0	Rope	1.2
○	Kill	Knife	0.8	Crime	3.1
	Ship	River	0.9	Water	2.2
	Window	Door	0.8	Glass	1.5
	Food	Beefsteak	1.0	Sashimi	1.3
○	Money	Banknote	0.7	Metal	3.5
	Cold	Water	1.1	Winter	2.3
	Illness	Cold	1.6	Tuberculosis	1.6
	Needle	Thread	1.0	Thread	1.2
○	Pine	Pot plant	0.8	Tree	2.3
	Mountain	High	0.9	River	1.4
○	Blood	Flow	1.0	Red	3.9
	New	Old	0.8	Clothes	2.1
	Hate	Spider	1.2	Illness	1.1
○	Pot	Pine	0.6	Flower	6.2
	Bird	Fly	0.9	Canary	3.6
	Book	Maruzen	1.0	Maruzen	1.3
○	Oiled paper	Hide	0.8	Package	4.0
	Friend	Saito	1.1	Talk	1.8
	Pure	Reason	1.2	Words	1.7
	Box	Bookshelf	1.0	Doll	1.2
○	Crime	Murder	0.7	Police	3.7
	Satisfaction	Completion	0.8	Family	2.0
	Woman	Government	1.0	Sister	1.3
	Picture	Screen	0.9	Landscape	1.3
○	Steal	Money	0.7	Horse	4.1

刺戟語	蕗屋清一郎		斎藤勇	
	反応語	所要時間	反応語	所要時間
頭	毛	0.9秒	尾	1.2秒
緑	青	0.7	青	1.1
水	湯	0.9	魚	1.3
歌う	唱歌	1.1	女	1.5
長い	短い	1.0	紐	1.2
○ 殺す	ナイフ	0.8	犯罪	3.1
舟	川	0.9	水	2.2
窓	戸	0.8	ガラス	1.5
料理	洋食	1.0	さしみ	1.3
○ 金	紙幣	0.7	鉄	3.5
冷い	水	1.1	冬	2.3
病気	風邪	1.6	肺病	1.6
針	糸	1.0	糸	1.2
○ 松	植木	0.8	木	2.3
山	高い	0.9	川	1.4
○ 血	流れる	1.0	赤い	3.9
新しい	古い	0.8	着物	2.1
嫌い	蜘蛛	1.2	病気	1.1
○ 植木鉢	松	0.6	花	6.2
鳥	飛ぶ	0.9	カナリヤ	3.6
本	丸善	1.0	丸善	1.3
○ 油紙	隠す	0.8	小包	4.0
友人	斎藤	1.1	話す	1.8
純粋	理性	1.2	言葉	1.7
箱	本箱	1.0	人形	1.2
○ 犯罪	人殺し	0.7	警察	3.7
満足	完成	0.8	家庭	2.0
女	政治	1.0	妹	1.3
絵	屏風	0.9	景色	1.3
○ 盗む	金	0.7	馬	4.1

The Psychological Examination

* Words marked with a ○ have some connection to the crime. For an actual test, two or three sets of a hundred are prepared and used in sequence; the table shown here is simplified for clarity.

"You see? Unusually clear, wouldn't you say?" the judge said after waiting for Akechi to glance over the records. "It looks from these results as if Saito is consciously crafting his responses in a number of ways. Most obviously when his response time slows, but this is not limited to words of interest—it lingers on to affect words that come immediately afterwards, and even some that come after that. What's more, given 'money' he responds 'metal'; given 'steal' he responds 'horse'—his associations are quite a stretch. His response to 'pot' took the longest of all, presumably because he had to push away both 'money' and 'pine.' By contrast, Fukiya's results are completely normal. His response to 'pot' is 'pine,' to 'oiled paper' 'hide,' to 'crime' 'murder': he calmly offers associations that the perpetrator would have to hide, and what is more he does so very quickly. For the murderer to show these responses would suggest severe feeblemindedness. On the contrary, though, Fukiya is in

★

■craft 動 〜を細工する　■linger 動 長引いて残る　■presumably 副 恐らく
■feeblemindedness 名 知的障害

＊ ○印は犯罪に関係ある単語。実際は百位使われるし、更にそれを二組も三組も用意して、次々と試験するのだが、右の表は解り易くする為めに簡単にしたものである。

「ね、非常に明瞭でしょう」判事は明智が記録に目を通すのを待って続けた「これで見ると、斎藤は色々故意の細工をやっている。一番よく分るのは反応時間の遅いことですが、それが問題の単語ばかりでなくその直ぐあとのや、二つ目のにまで影響しているのです。それから又、『金』に対して『鉄』と云ったり、『盗む』に対して『馬』といったり、可也無理な聯想をやってますよ、『植木鉢』に一番長くかかったのは、恐らく『金』と『松』という二つの聯想を押えつける為に手間取ったのでしょう。それに反して、蕗屋の方はごく自然です。『植木鉢』に『松』だとか、『油紙』に『隠す』だとか、『犯罪』に『人殺し』だとか、若し犯人だったら是非隠さなければならない様な聯想を平気で、而も短い時間に答えています。彼が人殺しの本人でいて、こんな反応を示したとすれば、余程の低能児に違いありません。ところが、実際は彼は――大学の学生で、それに却々秀才なのですからね」

The Psychological Examination

fact a student at — University, and a rather talented one at that."

"The results could be taken that way, yes."

Akechi's response came after considerable thought on something. The judge, however, did not notice Akechi's pointed expression, and pressed on.

"And yet. Even though these results leave no room for further doubt in Fukiya's case, on the matter of Saito's guilt I find myself unable to have full confidence, clear as the results of the examination are. Naturally, even if I declare him guilty at the pretrial hearing, that would not be the final judgment and so this level of confidence should suffice, but as you know I hate being wrong. Having my theories overturned at trial is irksome to me. And so, in fact, I remain in a state of uncertainty."

"These results are a fascinating sight," Akechi said, picking up the records. "Fukiya and Saito are both said to be rather dedicated scholars, and indeed in response to the word 'book,' both offer the name of the bookstore Maruzen; their characters show through clearly. What is more interesting is that while Fukiya's answers are all somehow substantial and rational, in Saito's there is something entirely gentle, is there not? A certain lyricism.

■pretrial hearing 予審　■suffice 動 〜に十分である　■irksome 形 イライラするような　■substantial 形 実体的な　■lyricism 名 叙情性

「そんな風にも取れますね」

明智は何か考え考え云った。併し判事は彼の意味あり気な表情には、少しも気附かないで、話を進めた。

「ところがですね。これで、もう蕗屋の方は疑う所はないのだが、斎藤が果して犯人かどうかという点になると、試験の結果はこんなにハッキリしているのに、どうも僕は確信が出来ないのですよ。何も予審で有罪にしたとて、それが最後の決定になる訳ではなし、まあこの位でいいのですが、御承知の様に僕は例のまけぬ気でね。公判で僕の考をひっくり返されるのが癪(しゃく)なんですよ。そんな訳で実はまだ迷っている始末です」

「これを見ると、実に面白いですね」明智が記録を手にして始めた。「蕗屋も斎藤も中々(なかなか)勉強家だって云いますが、『本』という単語に対して、両人共『丸善』と答えた所などは、よく性質が現れていますね。もっと面白いのは、蕗屋の答は、皆どことなく物質的で、理智的なのに反して、斎藤のは如何にもやさしい所があるじゃありませんか。叙情的ですね。例えば『女』だとか『着物』だとか『花』だとか『人形』だとか『景色』だとか『妹』だとかいう答は、どちらかと云えば、センチメンタルな弱々しい男を思わせま

The Psychological Examination

For example, 'woman,' or 'clothes,' or 'flower,' or 'doll,' or 'landscape,' or 'sister': such responses conjure up a rather sentimental and weak man. He appears to be rather sickly into the bargain: does he not respond to 'hate' with 'illness,' and to 'illness' with 'tuberculosis'? This is proof that he is haunted by the possibility of contracting that disease."

"That is one way to view the matter. It is in the nature of a free association test that the more one thinks on its results the more varied and interesting the conclusions that can emerge."

"Incidentally," said Akechi, changing his tone of voice somewhat, "I wonder how much thought you have given to the weaknesses of the association test. In criticizing the theories of Munsterberg, a proponent of psychological examination, De Quiros observes that although psychological testing was invented as a substitute for torture, results show that in fact it can condemn the innocent and overlook the guilty in the same way that torture did. Munsterberg himself writes somewhere to the effect that a psychological examination's true effectiveness is limited to uncovering whether a suspect knows a certain place, or person, or thing, and that its

★
■conjure up（イメージなどを）心に呼び起こす　■into the bargain　さらに
■tuberculosis 图結核　■be haunted by ～にさいなまれている　■proponent 图提唱者　■substitute for　～の代わりになる

すね。それから、斎藤はきっと病身ですよ。『嫌い』に『病気』と答え『病気』に『肺病』と答えてるじゃありませんか。平生から肺病になりはしないかと恐れてる証拠ですよ」

「そういう見方もありますね。聯想診断て奴は、考えれば考える丈け、色々面白い判断が出て来るものですよ」

「ところで」明智は少し口調を換えて云った。「あなたは、心理試験というものの弱点について考えられたことがありますかしら。デ・キロスは心理試験の提唱者ミュンスターベルヒの考を批評して、この方法は拷問に代るべく考案されたものだけれど、その結果は、やはり拷問と同じ様に、無辜のものを罪に陥れ、有罪者を逸することがあるといっていますね。ミュンスターベルヒ自身も、心理試験の真の効能は、嫌疑者が、ある場所とか、人とか、物について知っているかどうかを見出す場合に限って確定的だけれど、その他の場合には幾分危険だという様なことを、どっかで書いていました。あなたにこんな事を御話するのは釈迦に説法かも知れませんね。でも、これは確かに大切な点だと思いますが、どうでしょう」

The Psychological Examination

use can be dangerous in other situations. I suppose that speaking to you of such matters might be like 'preaching to the Buddha.' Still, this certainly strikes me as an important point. What do you think?"

"If one considers the bad cases, certainly. I know this as well, of course."

Mild displeasure showed in the judge's face as he spoke.

"However, we might find such bad cases of that sort surprisingly close at hand. Could one not argue as follows? Suppose that an innocent man of unusual nervous sensitivity is suspected of a crime. He is caught at the scene of the crime, and knows its facts well. In that case, would he be able to calmly face a psychological examination? Would it not be more natural for him to become somewhat exercised over the thought that he is being tested, and the question of how he should answer to avoid suspicion? This being so, would not a psychological test conducted under such circumstances become an instrument that 'condemns the innocent,' as de Quiros puts it?"

■preach 動説く ■strike ~ as ~に…という印象を与える ■close at hand すぐ手近に ■instrument 名手段

「それは悪い場合を考えれば、そうでしょうがね。無論僕もそれは知ってますよ」

判事は少しいやな顔をして答えた。

「併し、その悪い場合が、存外手近かにないとも限りませんからね。こういうことは云えないでしょうか。例えば、非常に神経過敏な、無辜の男が、ある犯罪の嫌疑を受けたと仮定しますね。その男は犯罪の現場を捕えられ、犯罪事実もよく知っているのです。この場合、彼は果して心理試験に対して平気でいることが出来るでしょうか。『ア、これは俺を試すのだな、どう答えたら疑われないだろう』などという風に亢奮するのが当然ではないでしょうか。ですから、そういう事情の下に行われた心理試験はデ・キロスの所謂『無辜のものを罪に陥れる』ことになりはしないでしょうか」

The Psychological Examination

"You are referring to Isamu Saito. Well, quite: it is precisely because I agree with you that I remain undecided in the manner I just explained, is it not?"

The sourness in the judge's expression grew.

"Well, then, if we suppose on those grounds that Saito is innocent of killing the old woman (although he must not, of course, escape punishment for stealing the money), who on earth did do it?"

Before Akechi was finished speaking, the judge broke in roughly with a question of his own.

"Well, then, do you have another candidate?"

"I do," Akechi replied with a smile. "To judge from these association test results, I believe that Fukiya is the culprit. I cannot declare it with certainty yet, but—I suppose he has already returned home. What do you think, would it be impossible to call him back here without offering a reason? If we could do that, I am sure that I would be able to pin down the truth for you."

"What did you say? Do you have any kind of proof of this?"

The judge was surprised to no small degree.

Without any suggestion of smugness, Akechi shared his thoughts with the judge in detail. The judge, in turn, was most impressed.

■sourness 图不機嫌　■break in 言葉を挟む　■candidate 图候補者　■pin down（事実などを）突き止める　■smugness 图得意げな様子

「君は斎藤勇のことを云っているのですね。イヤ、それは、僕も何となくそう感じたものだから、今も云った様に、まだ迷っているのじゃありませんか」
　判事は益々苦い顔をした。
「では、そういう風に、斎藤が無罪だとすれば（尤も金を盗んだ罪は免れませんけれど）一体誰が老婆を殺したのでしょう……」

　判事はこの明智の言葉を中途から引取って、荒々しく尋ねた。

「そんなら、君は、外に犯人の目当でもあるのですか」
「あります」明智がニコニコしながら答えた。「僕はこの聯想試験の結果から見て蕗屋が犯人だと思うのですよ。併しまだ確実にそうだとは云えませんけれど、あの男はもう帰宅したでしょうね。どうでしょう。それとなく彼をここへ呼ぶ訳には行きませんかしら、そうすれば、僕はきっと真相をつき止めて御目にかけますがね」

「なんですって。それには何か確かな証拠でもあるのですか」

　判事が少なからず驚いて尋ねた。
　明智は別に得意らしい色もなく、詳しく彼の考を述べた。そして、それが判事をすっかり感心させて了った。

The Psychological Examination

Akechi's hopes were granted, and a messenger was sent to Fukiya's lodgings.

Your friend Saito has in the end been found guilty. I would appreciate it if you would do me the favor of visiting my private residence to discuss certain matters in relation to this decision.

This was the content of the summons. Fukiya had just returned home from school when it arrived, and upon receiving the message set off for the judge's house at once. Even he was excited in no small degree at this good news. He was so overjoyed, in fact, that he did not even suspect the terrible trap that lay in store for him there.

VI

After explaining his reasons for finding Saito guilty, Judge Kasamori added a few words.

"I feel quite terrible for suspecting you. In fact, I had you come here today because I wanted to apologize as well as explain the situation."

■be found guilty 有罪を宣告される　■do ~ a favor ～に手を貸す　■set off for ～に出かける　■in store for ～を待ち構えて

明智の希望が容れられて、蕗屋の下宿へ使が走った。

「御友人の斎藤氏は愈々有罪と決した。それについて御話したいこともあるから、私の私宅まで御足労を煩し度い」

これが呼出しの口上だった。蕗屋は丁度学校から帰った所で、それを聞くと早速やって来た。流石の彼もこの吉報には少からず興奮していた。嬉しさの余り、そこに恐ろしい罠のあることを、まるで気附かなかった。

六

笠森判事は、一通り斎藤を有罪と決定した理由を説明したあとで、こう附加えた。
「君を疑ったりして、全く相済まんと思っているのです。今日は、実はそのお詫び旁々、事情をよくお話しようと思って、来て頂いた訳ですよ」

The Psychological Examination

He then ordered that tea be brought in for Fukiya and engaged him in light conversation, allowing an entirely relaxed air to pervade the gathering. Akechi joined the discussion as well. The judge introduced him as a lawyer of his acquaintance who had been engaged by the old woman's heirs to collect her debts and so forth. Of course, half of this was a lie, but it was true that after a family meeting it had been decided that the old woman's nephew would come up from the country to execute her estate.

The conversation between the three of them covered a range of topics, beginning with rumors about Saito. Now entirely confident of his position, Fukiya was the most loquacious of the group.

Time passed in this manner until the approach of evening became visible through the windows outside. Happening to notice how late it was getting, Fukiya began his preparations to leave as he spoke.

"Well, I must be off. Was there anything else you wanted to discuss?"

"Oh, I almost forgot!" Akechi said cheerfully. "It's nothing, really, but since you're here…. I'm not sure if you knew or not, but there was a two-paneled gold-leaf

★

■pervade 動（雰囲気などが）広がる　■heir 名相続者　■and so forth 〜など
■loquacious 形おしゃべりな

そして、蕗屋の為には紅茶を命じたりして極く打ちくつろいだ様子で雑談を始めた。明智も話に加わった。判事は、彼を知合の弁護士で、死んだ老婆の遺産相続者から、貸金の取立て等を依頼されている男だといって紹介した。無論半分は嘘だけれども親族会議の結果、老婆の甥が田舎から出て来て、遺産を相続することになったのは事実だった。

　三人の間には、斎藤の噂を始めとして、色々の話題が話された。すっかり安心した蕗屋は、中でも一番雄弁な話手だった。

　そうしている内に、いつの間にか時間が経って、窓の外に夕暗が迫って来た。蕗屋はふとそれに気附くと、帰り支度を始めながら云った。

「では、もう失礼しますが、別に御用はないでしょうか」

「オオ、すっかり忘れて了うところだった」明智が快活に云った。「なあに、どうでもいい様なことですがね。丁度序だから、……御承知かどうですか、あの殺人のあった部屋に、二枚折りの金

The Psychological Examination

painted screen in the room where the murder took place, and a problem has arisen around some slight damage to it. The issue is that the screen didn't belong to the old woman; she was merely holding it as collateral, and now its true owner is demanding compensation for the damage, which he says must have been done during the murder. But the old woman's nephew—as miserly as his aunt—refuses to comply, insisting that the damage might have been there before. A tiresome problem, but one that is giving us some difficulty. The screen does seem to have been quite a valuable item, though. Now, you were often in and out of that house so I suspect that you were familiar with the screen I mean. Do you have any memory of whether the damage was there before? What do you say? I'm sure you didn't pay it much attention, a painted screen like that. We actually asked Saito as well, but the chap was so worked up he couldn't be sure. We even tried to ask the maid, but she has returned to her home prefecture and we weren't able to clarify the matter through correspondence, which leaves us in a bit of a pickle…"

It was true that the screen had been collateral, but the other points were, of course, fiction and nothing more. Hearing the word "screen" had given Fukiya chills.

★

■collateral 名抵当　■compensation 名補償、弁償　■miserly 形けちな
■pickle 名困った立場

屏風が立ててあったのですが、それに一寸傷がついていたと云って問題になっているのですよ。というのは、その屏風は婆さんのものではなく、貸金の抵当に預ってあった品で、持主の方では、殺人の際についた傷に相違ないから弁償しろというし、婆さんの甥は、これが又婆さんに似たけちん坊でね、元からあった傷かも知れないといって、却々応じないのです。実際つまらない問題で、閉口してるんです。尤もその屏風は可也値うちのある品物らしいのですけれど。ところで、あなたはよくあの家へ出入りされたのですから、その屏風も多分御存じでしょうが、以前に傷があったかどうか、ひょっと御記憶じゃないでしょうか。どうでしょう。屏風なんか別に注意しなかったでしょうね。実は斎藤にも聞いて見たんですが、先生亢奮し切っていて、よく分らないのです、それに、女中は国へ帰って了って、手紙で聞合せても要領を得ないし、一寸困っているのですが……」

　屏風が抵当物だったことはほんとうだが、その外の点は無論作り話に過ぎなかった。蕗屋は屏風という言葉に思わずヒヤッとした。

The Psychological Examination

Having heard Akechi out, however, and learned that there was nothing to worry about, Fukiya relaxed again. *Why should I still be on edge? The case is closed for good!*

Fukiya briefly considered how to answer Akechi's question. It seemed to him that here, too, artlessness would be the best policy.

"As the judge knows, I have only entered that room once. Even that was just two days before the incident."

Fukiya smirked as he spoke. To speak of the matter in such terms was simply too delicious.

"I do remember that screen, though. It wasn't damaged when I saw it."

"Is that so? Are you quite sure? It's only a tiny little tear, just over Ono no Komachi's face."

"Ah, yes, now I remember," Fukiya said, acting as if he had suddenly recalled some new information. "The screen had a painting of the Six Saints of Poetry on it, didn't it? I remember Ono no Komachi. But if the screen had been damaged at that time, I would surely have noticed. A tear on that vivid Komachi's face would have been apparent at a glance."

★

■hear ~ out ～の話を最後まで聞く　■on edge ビクビクして　■for good 永久に　■artlessness 率直さ　■delicious 非常に面白い　■apparent すぐに分かる

併しよく聞いて見ると何でもないことなので、すっかり安心した。「何をビクビクしているのだ。事件はもう落着して了ったのじゃないか」

　彼はどんな風に答えてやろうかと、一寸思案したが、例によってありのままにやるのが一番いい方法の様に考えられた。

「判事さんはよく御承知ですが、僕はあの部屋へ入ったのはたった一度切りなんです。それも、事件の二日前にね」
　彼はニヤニヤ笑いながら云った。こうした云い方をするのが愉快でたまらないのだ。
「併し、その屏風なら覚えてますよ。僕の見た時には確か傷なんかありませんでした」
「そうですか。間違いないでしょうね。あの小野の小町の顔の所に、ほんの一寸した傷がある丈けなんですが」
「そうそう、思出しましたよ」蕗屋は如何にも今思出した風を装って云った。
「あれは六歌仙の絵でしたね。小野の小町も覚えてますよ。併し、もしその時傷がついていたとすれば、見落した筈がありません。だって、極彩色の小町の顔に傷があれば、一目で分りますからね」

The Psychological Examination

"In that case, I wonder if I might impose on you to offer a statement on the matter. The owner of the screen is a man of remarkable greed and quite intractable."

"Certainly. Whenever it is convenient for you."

Fukiya granted the request to the man he believed a lawyer with a certain condescension.

"Thank you," Akechi said, looking pleased as he ran his fingers through his unruly hair. This was a kind of tic that appeared when he was worked up about something. "In fact, I suspected all along that you would surely know about the screen. 'Screen' was your rather unusual response to 'picture' in yesterday's examination, after all. That was what tipped me off. Painted screens are seldom counted among the furnishings in student lodgings, and you did not seem to have any particularly close friends other than Saito, so I imagined that *for some reason* the screen in the old woman's drawing room must have left an especially deep impression on you."

Fukiya was mildly surprised. Of course, everything the lawyer had said was correct. But why had he let "screen" slip out of his mouth yesterday? And was it not dangerous that he had mysteriously not noticed this at all until just now? On the other hand, where might that danger lie?

★

■greed 名強欲　■intractable 形手に負えない　■with condescension 恩着せがましい　■tic 名癖　■tipp ~ off ~に情報をほのめかす　■count among ~に属するものとみなす

「じゃ御迷惑でも、証言をして頂く訳には行きませんかしら、屏風の持主というのが、実に慾の深い奴で始末にいけないのですよ」

「エエ、よござんすとも、いつでも御都合のいい時に」
　蕗屋はいささか得意になって、弁護士と信ずる男の頼みを承諾した。
　「ありがとう」明智はモジャモジャに延ばした頭を指でかき廻しながら、嬉し相に云った。これは、彼が多少亢奮した際にやる一種の癖なのだ。「実は、僕は最初から、あなたが屏風のことを知って居られるに相違ないと思ったのですよ。というのはね、この昨日の心理試験の記録の中で『絵』という問に対して、あなたは『屏風』という特別の答え方をしていますね。これですよ。下宿屋にはあんまり屏風なんて備えてありませんし、あなたは斎藤の外には別段親しいお友達もない様ですから、これはさしずめ老婆の座敷の屏風が、何かの理由で特別に深い印象になって残っていたのだろうと想像したのですよ」

　蕗屋は一寸驚いた。それは確かにこの弁護士のいう通りに相違なかった。でも、彼は昨日どうして屏風なんてことを口走ったのだろう。そして、不思議にも今までまるでそれに気附かないとは、これは危険じゃないかな。併し、どういう点が危険なのだろう。あの時彼は、その傷跡をよく検べて、何の手掛りにもならぬこと

The Psychological Examination

Had he not examined the tear on the screen carefully at the time, confirming that it would be of no use as a clue? Everything was fine, just fine, he thought, and relaxed again.

In fact, however, he was without realizing it committing the gravest of errors, one which made the truth all too clear.

"I see. I didn't notice at all, myself, but it is just as you say. I doff my cap at your powers of observation, sir."

Fukiya remained calm, not forgetting to maintain his policy of guileless simplicity.

"Oh, it just happened to catch my eye," the alleged lawyer Akechi said modestly. "But speaking of things I noticed, there was another—oh, nothing to worry about, of course. There were eight dangerous words in yesterday's free association test, and you passed them perfectly. *Too* perfectly, in fact. If you had any shameful secrets, things would not have gone so well. The eight words are marked with a circle here, do you see? Take a look." Akechi showed Fukiya the results as he spoke. "Your response times for these items were all even faster than your response to the meaningless words, albeit by the tiniest of margins. For example, your reply of 'pine'

★

■doff one's cap 〜に敬意を評して帽子を脱ぐ　■guileless 形 率直な　■alleged 形 〜とされている　■albeit 接 〜にもかかわらず　■margin 名 (時間の) 差

を確めて置いたではないか。なあに、平気だ平気だ。彼は一応考えて見てやっと安心した。

　ところが、ほんとうは、彼は明白すぎる程明白な大間違をやっていたことを少しも気がつかなかったのだ。

「なる程、僕はちっとも気附きませんでしたけれど、確かにおっしゃる通りですよ。却々鋭い御観察ですね」
　蘆屋は、あくまで無技巧主義を忘れないで平然として答えた。

「なあに、偶然気附いたのですよ」弁護士を装った明智が謙遜した。「だが、気附いたと云えば実はもう一つあるのですが、イヤ、イヤ、決して御心配なさる様なことじゃありません。昨日の聯想試験の中には八つの危険な単語が含まれていたのですが、あなたはそれを実に完全にパスしましたね。実際完全すぎた程ですよ。少しでも後暗い所があれば、こうは行きませんからね。その八つの単語というのは、ここに丸が打ってあるでしょう。これですよ」といって明智は記録の紙片を示した。「ところが、あなたのこれらに対する反応時間は、外の無意味な言葉よりも、皆、ほんの僅かずつではありますけれど、早くなってますね。例えば、『植木鉢』に対して『松』と答えるのに、たった〇・六秒しかかかってない。これは珍らしい無邪気さですよ。この三十箇の単語の内で、一番

The Psychological Examination

in response to 'pot' took you just 0.6 seconds. Such guilelessness is rare. Among these thirty words, the easiest association is surely 'blue' in response to 'green,' but you took 0.7 seconds even for that."

Fukiya began to feel exceedingly uneasy. Why was this lawyer so talkative?

Out of goodwill, or of malice? Could some secret motivation underlie his words? Fukiya strove with all his might to grasp the import of what Akechi said.

"'Pot,' 'oiled paper,' 'crime,' and the rest of the eight problem words—it's certainly impossible to believe that associations came easier for those than for unremarkable words like 'head' and 'green.' And yet, your replies to the difficult words were actually faster. What can this mean? This, then, is the other thing I noticed. May I make an attempt to guess at your mental state? Everything is worth trying once. I apologize in advance for any errors, of course."

Fukiya shivered. However, what had caused this was unclear even to him.

"You knew the dangers of the psychological examination well, and had prepared for it in advance. Regarding the words related to the crime, you had

■exceedingly 副 非常に   ■out of goodwill 好意によって   ■strive with all one's might 全力を傾ける   ■mental state 心理状況

聯想し易いのは先ず『緑』に対する『青』などでしょうが、あなたはそれにさえ〇・七秒かかってますからね」

　蕗屋は非常な不安を感じ始めた。この弁護士は、一体何の為にこんな饒舌を弄しているのだろう。
　好意でかそれとも悪意でか。何か深い下心があるのじゃないかしら。彼は全力を傾けて、その意味を悟ろうとした。

　「『植木鉢』にしろ『油紙』にしろ『犯罪』にしろ、その外、問題の八つの単語は、皆、決して『頭』だとか『緑』だとかいう平凡なものよりも聯想し易いとは考えられません。それにも拘らず、あなたは、その難しい聯想の方を却って早く答えているのです。これはどういう意味でしょう。僕が気づいた点というのはここですよ。一つ、あなたの心持を当てて見ましょうか、エ、どうです。何も一興ですからね。併し若し間違っていたら御免下さいよ」

　蕗屋はブルッと身震いした。併し、何がそうさせたかは彼自身にも分らなかった。
　「あなたは、心理試験の危険なことをよく知っていて、予め準備していたのでしょう。犯罪に関係のある言葉について、ああ云えばこうと、ちゃんと腹案が出来ていたんでしょう。イヤ、僕は

The Psychological Examination

decided in advance that if such-and-such a word came up, you would say so-and-so. —No, no, I do not intend this as criticism of your approach. It is true that psychological examinations can, depending on circumstances, be extremely dangerous, after all. One cannot be certain that they will not 'overlook the guilty and condemn the innocent.' It's just that your preparations were so comprehensive that although of course you had no intention of replying more quickly, associations for those words alone became faster. This was a terrible mistake, was it not? You were so worried about being too slow that you did not realize that the same danger lay in being too fast. Of course, the difference in time was so slight that an observer would miss it entirely unless they were paying very close attention. In any case, a dissimulation always has flaws somewhere." This point alone was the basis of Akechi's suspicion of Fukiya. "Why, however, did you choose to reply with words likely to attract suspicion, like 'money,' 'murder,' and 'hide'? The answer is obvious: This was your *innocence* at work. If you were the killer, you certainly would not reply to 'oiled paper' with 'hide,' after all. That you calmly provided replies so dangerous to you is itself proof that you had nothing to hide. What say you? Do I have it correctly?"

■such-and-such 形あれこれの　■so-and-so 名しかじか　■comprehensive 形広範囲の　■flaw 名欠陥、ひび

決して、あなたのやり方を非難するのではありませんよ。実際、心理試験という奴は、場合によっては非常に危険なものですからね。有罪者を逸して無辜のものを罪に陥れることがないとは断言出来ないのですからね。ところが、準備があまり行届き過ぎていて、勿論、別に早く答える積りはなかったのでしょうけれど、その言葉丈けが早くなって了ったのです。これは確かに大変な失敗でしたね。あなたは、ただもう遅れることばかり心配して、それが早過ぎるのも同じ様に危険だということを少しも気づかなかったのです。尤も、その時間の差は非常に僅かずつですから、余程注意深い観察者でないとうっかり見逃して了いますがね。兎に角、拵え事というものは、どっかに破綻があるものですよ」明智の蕗屋を疑った論拠は、ただこの一点にあったのだ。「併し、あなたはなぜ、『金』だとか『人殺し』だとか『隠す』だとか、嫌疑を受け易い言葉を選んで答えたのでしょう。云うまでもない。そこがそれ、あなたの無邪気な所ですよ。若しあなたが犯人だったら、決して『油紙』と問われて『隠す』などとは答えませんからね。そんな危険な言葉を平気で答え得るのは何等やましい所のない証拠ですよ。ね、そうでしょう。僕のいう通りでしょう」

The Psychological Examination

Fukiya was staring into Akechi's eyes. For some reason, he was unable to look away. Below his nose, the muscles around his mouth had gone stiff; he felt as if he could neither laugh, nor cry, nor express surprise or any other emotion.

Nor, of course, could he talk. If he had tried to force himself to, what came out would surely have turned immediately into a scream of terror.

"That innocence, which is to say absence of artifice, is a highly recognizable characteristic of yours. I asked you those questions because I knew this to be true. Come, do you not see? The painted screen! I believed without doubt that you would reply truthfully. And so you did. But, allow me to ask this of Judge Kasamori: When was the painting screen in question brought into the old woman's house?"

Akechi turned to the judge, feigning uncertainty.

"The day before the murder. The fourth of last month."

"What—the day before? Truly? How strange! Fukiya has just told us that two days before the incident, which is to say on the third, he saw the screen in that room. He was quite clear on the matter. This makes no sense at all. One of you must be mistaken."

■look away 目をそらす　■go stiff 緊張して硬くなる　■artifice 小細工
■feign 〜のふりをする　■make no sense 理にかなわない

蕗屋は話手の目をじっと見詰めていた。どういう訳か、そらすことが出来ないのだ。そして、鼻から口の辺にかけて筋肉が硬直して、笑うことも、泣くことも、驚くことも、一切の表情が不可能になった様な気がした。

　無論口は利けなかった。もし無理に口を利こうとすれば、それは直ちに恐怖の叫声になったに相違ない。

「この無邪気なこと、つまり小細工を弄しないということが、あなたの著(いちじる)しい特徴ですよ。僕はそれを知ったものだから、あの様な質問をしたのです。エ、お分りになりませんか。例の屏風のことです。僕は、あなたが無論無邪気にありのままにお答え下さることを信じて疑わなかったのですよ。実際その通りでしたがね。ところで、笠森さんに伺いますが、問題の六歌仙の屏風は、いつあの老婆の家に持込まれたのですかしら」
　明智はとぼけた顔をして、判事に聞いた。
「犯罪事件の前日ですよ。つまり先月の四日です」

「エ、前日ですって、それは本当ですか。妙じゃありませんか、今蕗屋君は、事件の前々日即ち三日に、それをあの部屋で見たと、ハッキリ云っているじゃありませんか。どうも不合理ですね。あなた方のどちらかが間違っていないとしたら」

The Psychological Examination

"I suppose Fukiya is misremembering," the judge said with a grin.

"We can be certain, then, that until the evening of the fourth, that screen was at the residence of its true owner."

Akechi observed Fukiya's expression with deep interest. It had begun to crumple up oddly, like that of a little girl about to burst into tears.

This was the trap Akechi had planned to set from the beginning. He had heard from the judge that the screen had not been in the old woman's house two days before the murder.

"We appear to have struck a problem," Akechi said, in a voice expressing befuddlement. "This is a blunder too large to overcome. Why did you claim to have seen something that you could not, in fact, have seen? You are not supposed to have visited the house once since two days before the accident. But it is remembering the picture of the Six Poetic Saints that strikes the critical blow. Perhaps in your eagerness to tell the truth, you accidentally told a lie—is that it? When you entered the drawing room two days before the incident, did you pay attention to whether there was a painted screen there or not? You did not, of course—it had no connection to your plan, and even if there had been a screen there, as you know it would have

■grin 図ニヤっと笑うこと　■crumple up クシャクシャにする　■burst into tears ワッと泣き出す　■befuddlement 図困惑　■blunder 図大失敗

「蕗屋君は何か思違いをしているのでしょう」判事がニヤニヤ笑いながら云った。

「四日の夕方まではあの屏風は、そのほんとうの持主の所にあったことが、明白に判っているのです」

明智は深い興味を以て、蕗屋の表情を観察した。それは、今にも泣き出そうとする小娘の顔の様に変な風にくずれかけていた。

これが明智の最初から計画した罠だった。彼は事件の二日前には、老婆の家に屏風のなかったことを、判事から聞いて知っていたのだ。

「どうも困ったことになりましたね」明智はさも困った様な声音で云った「これはもう取返しのつかぬ大失策ですよ。なぜあなたは見もしないものを見たなどと云うのです。あなたは事件の二日前から一度もあの家へ行っていない筈じゃありませんか。殊に六歌仙の絵を覚えていたのは、致命傷ですよ。恐らくあなたは、ほんとうのことを云おう、ほんとうのことを云おうとして、つい嘘をついて了ったのでしょう。ね、そうでしょう。あなたは事件の二日前にあの座敷へ入った時、そこに屏風があるかないかという様なことを注意したでしょうか。無論注意しなかったでしょう。実際それは、あなたの計画には何の関係もなかったのですし、若し屏風があったとしても、あれは御承知の通り時代のついたくすんだ色合で、他の色々な道具類の中で殊更ら目立っていた訳でもありませんからね。で、あなたが今、事件の当日そこで見た屏風

The Psychological Examination

been aged and dark, not standing out in particular among the other goods of the house. Now, it is entirely natural for you to assume that the screen you saw on the day of the incident must have been there two days earlier as well. And, of course, I asked you in a way intended to make you think so. This is a kind of illusion, but one that is abundant in our day-to-day lives if one gives the matter some consideration. Still, had you been a normal criminal, you would never have replied in the way you did. Criminals believe it best to hide everything, you see. How fortunate for me that your mind is ten times, twenty times more advanced than that of the average judge or criminal! In other words, you believed that as long as your weak points remained untouched, it would be safest simply to speak as naturally as possible. Keeping one step ahead of the psychological examination, you might say. But I explored one step beyond even that. You never imagined for a moment, I am sure, that a lawyer unconnected to the case might be setting a trap designed to force you to confess. Ha ha ha ha ha!"

Fukiya's face had gone quite pale and his forehead was damp with sweat. He remained silent. At this point, he reasoned, the more he tried to defend himself the more exposed he would be.

■abundant 形 たくさんある　■day-to-day 形 日常の　■keep one step ahead of 〜を一歩先んじる、〜の裏をかく　■be damp with sweat 汗で湿っている

が、二日前にも同じ様にそこにあっただろうと考えたのは、ごく自然ですよ。それに僕はそう思わせる様な方法で問いかけたのですものね。これは一種の錯覚見たいなものですが、よく考えて見ると、我々には日常ザラにあることです。併し、もし普通の犯罪者だったら決してあなたの様には答えなかったでしょう。彼等は、何でもかんでも、隠しさえすればいいと思っているのですからね。ところが、僕にとって好都合だったのは、あなたが世間並みの裁判官や犯罪者より、十倍も二十倍も進んだ頭を持っていられたことです。つまり、急所にふれない限りは、出来る丈けあからさまに喋って了う方が、却って安全だという信念を持っていられたことです。裏の裏を行くやり方ですね。そこで僕は更らにその裏を行って見たのですよ。まさか、あなたはこの事件に何の関係もない弁護士が、あなたを白状させる為に、罠を作っていようとは想像しなかったでしょうね。ハハハハハ」

　蕗屋は、真青になった顔の、額の所にビッショリ汗を浮かせて、じっと黙り込んでいた。彼はもうこうなったら、弁明すればする丈け、ボロを出す許りだと思った。

The Psychological Examination

An intelligent man, Fukiya grasped well how eloquent a confession his slip must have been. Mysteriously, in his mind's eye he saw scenes from his childhood appear and disappear like a spinning lantern.

There was a long silence.

"Do you hear that?" Akechi said at last. "There. That scribbling sound. Do you know what that is? Right from the start, I had someone in the next room transcribing our conversation.... You can come out now! Please bring the transcript with you."

A paper screen slid to one side and a man with the air of a student emerged carrying a sheaf of Western-style notepaper.

"Please read that aloud for us."

Obeying Akechi's order, the man read the transcript through from beginning to end.

"Well, Fukiya, will you sign and seal this for me? Your thumbprint will do. I'm sure you won't refuse. Why, didn't you promise only a few minutes ago to make a statement about the painted screen whenever it was convenient for me? Little suspecting what sort of statement it would be, of course."

Fukiya knew well that there was nothing to be gained

❖

■scribble 動走り書きする　■right from the start 最初から　■air of ～風の
■sign and steal 署名押印する　■thumbprint 拇母印

彼は、頭がいい丈けに、自分の失言がどんなに雄弁な自白だったかということを、よく弁えていた。彼の頭の中には、妙なことだが、子供の時分からの様々の出来事が、走馬燈の様に、めまぐるしく現れては消えた。
　長い沈黙が続いた。
　「聞えますか」明智が暫くしてから云った。「そら、サラサラ、サラサラという音がしているでしょう。あれはね。最前から、隣の部屋で、僕達の問答を書きとめているのですよ。……君、もうようござんすから、それをここへ持って来て呉れませんか」

　すると、襖が開いて、一人の書生体の男が手に洋紙の束を持って出て来た。

　「それを一度読み上げて下さい」
　明智の命令に随って、その男は最初から朗読した。

　「では、蕗屋君、これに署名して、拇印で結構ですから捺して呉れませんか。君はまさかいやだとは云いますまいね。だって、さっき、屏風のことはいつでも証言してやると約束したばかりじゃありませんか。尤も、こんな風な証言だろうとは想像しなかったかも知れないけれど」

　蕗屋は、ここで署名を拒んだところで、何の甲斐もないことを、

The Psychological Examination

from refusing to sign at this point. Partly out of respect for Akechi's astonishing deduction, he signed and sealed the document. Then his posture sagged into the droop of one who has completely given up.

"As I said earlier," Akechi explained in closing, "Munsterberg writes that the psychological examination's true reliability is limited to uncovering whether a suspect knows a certain place, or person, or thing. In terms of this case, the point was whether Fukiya had seen the painted screen. If this point were ignored, a hundred psychological examinations would surely have been useless. After all, our adversary was Fukiya: a man who anticipates everything and prepares meticulously for it. One other thing I would like to mention is that psychological examinations do not necessarily require a list of stimulus words made according to the directions in a book, or specialized equipment. They can also be performed entirely through casual conversation, as I have shown in this examination here. Indeed, since the days of yore, great judges such as Ooka, the Governor of Echizen, have used the very methods recently discovered by the field of psychology—without even realizing that they were doing so."

■deduction 名 推理　■sag 動 元気をなくす　■droop 名 うなだれること　■adversary 名 (対戦の) 相手　■meticulously 副 綿密に準備して　■days of yore 昔

十分知っていた。彼は明智の驚くべき推理をも、併せて承認する意味で、署名捺印した。そして、今はもうすっかりあきらめ果てた人の様にうなだれていた。

「先にも申上げた通り」明智は最後に説明した。「ミュンスターベルヒは、心理試験の真の効能は、嫌疑者が、ある場所、人又は物について知っているかどうかを試す場合に限って確定的だといっています。今度の事件で云えば、蕗屋君が屏風を見たかどうかという点が、それなんです。この点を外にしては、百の心理試験も恐らく無駄でしょう。何しろ、相手が蕗屋君の様な、何もかも予想して、綿密な準備をしている男なのですからね。それからもう一つ申上げ度いのは、心理試験というものは、必ずしも、書物に書いてある通り一定の刺戟語を使い、一定の機械を用意しなければ出来ないものではなくて、今僕が実験してお目にかけた通り、極く日常的な会話によってでも、十分やれるということです。昔からの名判官は、例えば大岡越前守という様な人は、皆自分でも気づかないで、最近の心理学が発明した方法を、ちゃんと応用しているのですよ」

確かな読解のための英語表現［文法］

that（形容詞、関係代名詞、同格、強調構文、慣用表現）

品詞も用法も実にさまざまなthat。読んでいて「いったいどの用法、どの意味だろう」と混乱してしまい、次に進めなくなることがありませんか。一見、読解が複雑に見えるthatですが、用法がわかってしまえば「あのthat」か、と見当がつき、さらに深くストーリーに入りこむことができます。ここで見てみましょう。

> In <u>that</u> part of the city, every street was of the same quiet residential sort.（p.214, 下から4行目）
> その一劃はどの通りも淋しい屋敷町だった。

【解説】まずは形容詞「あの」のthatからです。「街のその部分」の「その」に当たるthatです。

> He did not have any equipment <u>that</u> could measure microscopic changes,（p.244, 3行目）
> 微細な変化を計る道具がある訳ではない

【解説】関係代名詞のthatが主格で用いられています。whichと同じ用法ですが、先行詞が強く限定される場合には、thatが用いられることが比較的多いと言えます。ここでは、thatの前のequipmentが先行詞で、「〜を測ることのできる道具」という意味になります。not…any「まったくない」という強い意味がequipmentに加えられているため、関係代名詞としてwhichではなくthatが用いられたと考えられます。

> He often took his walk in this area, and could simply say that he had been out for a walk on the day in question as well. (p.204, 下から5行目)
>
> 彼はよく其辺を散歩することがあるのだから、当日も散歩をしたばかりだと云い抜けることが出来る。

【解説】もっとも頻繁に見る用法のthatがおそらくこれでしょう。sayの目的語となるthat節を構成しています。「問題の日に散歩していたのだと、単にそう言えばいいのだ」という意味になります。as wellは、前の文this would cause no difficulty「まったく問題ではないだろう」を受けて「これも同様（に問題ないだろう）」の意味を付加しています。

> He made frequent mention of her savings and the rumor that she had hidden them somewhere, watching her eyes closely each time he said the word "hidden." (p.202, 4行目)
>
> 屡々老婆の財産のこと、それを彼女がどこかへ隠しているという噂のあることなぞ口にした。

【解説】同格のthatです。thatはthe rumorの同格で「～という噂」です。なお、このthe rumorは、andの前のfrequent mention ofからつながっています。mention of her savings and of the rumorで「財産と噂について口にする」となります。

> it is true that he lamented the fact that the extent to which he could read and think as he pleased was limited by the need to spend time on trivial piecework to pay his expenses.
> （p.188, 8行目）
>
> 学資を得る為に、つまらぬ内職に時を取られて、好きな読書や思索が十分出来ないのを残念に思っていたのは確かだ。
>
> It is true that psychological examinations can, depending on circumstances, be extremely dangerous, after all. （p.286, 3行目）
> 実際、心理試験という奴は、場合によっては非常に危険なものですからね。

【解説】ここに挙げた2つは、形式主語itを受ける真主語である名詞節を導く従位接続詞のthatです。1文目にはthatが2つありますが、最初のthatがこの用法です。that以下が主語で、この前のtrueが補語、「〜は真実だ」という意味です。the factの後のthatは、この前に説明した同格のthatで「〜というのは事実だ」です。that節の中の主語はthe extent「度合い」で、述語動詞は少し先のwas limited「度合いが制限される」のが文の骨格です。

　2文目のthatも、that以下が主語でtrueが補語です。この文にはコンマが3つあります。最初と2番目は「挿入」を表すコンマで、慣れないうちはこの中を除いて読み、後から戻ってくればよいでしょう。「状況に応じて」の意味です。

> It is in the nature of a free association test that the more one thinks on its results the more varied and interesting the conclusions that can emerge. （p.266, 8行目）
> 聯想診断て奴は、考えれば考える丈け、色々面白い判断が出て来るものですよ。

【解説】強調構文のit is…thatです。文の要素として、重要な箇所（強調したいところ）をit is…thatで挟み、その他の要素をthatの後に続ける用法です。ここではin the nature of a free association「連想診断の性質」が、強調される要素です。

強調構文を見分けるには、it isとthatを抜いて考えます。この３語がなくても文として成立すれば、それは強調構文。文の要素が何か足りなければ、強調構文ではなく、関係代名詞や同格のthatです。

　この文はちょっと長いので直訳すると「連想診断の性質というものは、その結果について考えれば考えるほど、そこから得られる結論は多様で興味深い」となります。この文にはさらに、the比較級〜 , the比較級の表現も用いられています。「〜すればするほど…だ」という意味です。

> It went without saying that practice was just as necessary for examinations of this type as it was for the types mentioned earlier.（p.250, 下から4行目）
> この種の試験に対しては、前の場合と同じく「練習」が必要なのは云うまでもない。

【解説】用法としては形式主語のitの内容を説明するthatですが、It goes without saying that 〜で「〜は言うまでもない」という意味の慣用表現です。goesが過去形になっているのに注意しましょう。

E-CATとは…
英語が話せるようになるためのテストです。インターネットベースで、30分であなたの発話力をチェックします。

www.ecatexam.com

iTEP®とは…
世界各国の企業、政府機関、アメリカの大学300校以上が、英語能力判定テストとして採用。オンラインによる90分のテストで文法、リーディング、リスニング、ライティング、スピーキングの5技能をスコア化。iTEP®は、留学、就職、海外赴任などに必要な、世界に通用する英語力を総合的に評価する画期的なテストです。

www.itepexamjapan.com

[IBC対訳ライブラリー]
英語で読む江戸川乱歩短篇集

2016年9月4日　第1刷発行

著　者　　江戸川乱歩

発行者　　浦　晋亮

発行所　　IBCパブリッシング株式会社
　　　　　〒162-0804 東京都新宿区中里町29番3号 菱秀神楽坂ビル9F
　　　　　Tel. 03-3513-4511　Fax. 03-3513-4512
　　　　　www.ibcpub.co.jp

印刷所　　株式会社シナノパブリッシングプレス

© IBC Publishing, Inc. 2016

Printed in Japan

落丁本・乱丁本は、小社宛にお送りください。送料小社負担にてお取り替えいたします。
本書の無断複写（コピー）は著作権法上での例外を除き禁じられています。

ISBN978-4-7946-0432-3